SHOOTING THE COOK

DAVID PRITCHARD

SHOOTING THE COOK

A TRUE STORY ABOUT FOOD, TELEVISION AND THE RISE OF TV'S SUPERCHEFS – THE DIRECTOR'S CUT

FOURTH ESTATE · *London*

First published in Great Britain by
Fourth Estate
A division of HarperCollins*Publishers*
77–85 Fulham Palace Road
London W6 8JB
www.4thestate.co.uk
Love this book? www.bookarmy.com

1

A catalogue record for this book is available from the British Library

ISBN 978-0-00-727830-5

Typeset in Adobe Caslon by
G&M Designs Limited, Raunds, Northamptonshire

Printed in Great Britain by Clays Ltd, St Ives plc

Mixed Sources
Product group from well-managed
forests and other controlled sources
www.fsc.org Cert no. SW-COC-1806
© 1996 Forest Stewardship Council
FSC

FSC is a non-profit international organisation established to promote the
responsible management of the world's forests. Products carrying the FSC
label are independently certified to assure consumers that they come
from forests that are managed to meet the social, economic and
ecological needs of present or future generations.

Find out more about HarperCollins and the environment at
www.harpercollins.co.uk/green

To Jane, who forced me to write this;
to Prudence, my English bull terrier, for being
such an inspiration on walks, and to my mother,
who is the best cook in the world.

*Over the years there has been the odd
fleeting moment when I'd have eagerly
swapped the camera for a revolver.*

Contents

Foreword

David read the first chapter of his memoirs to us in the film crew van while we were waiting for a tiny rusty ferry to take us from Haiphong to Cat Ba Island, one of the 367 islands of the Cat Ba Archipelago in Ha Long Bay, Vietnam. It took about five boats to get us there, a voyage of a mile or so to one island then a short drive to an even smaller boat on the other side of the island. We had plenty of time to listen. There was nothing else to do, certainly nothing to buy, only purple, green, or orange soft drinks on sale in dusty bottles at the kiosks on the slipways. We were all laughing so much after the first couple of pages anyway. He really wasn't being self-effacing. His early days in TV were chaotic and his first cookery series with Keith Floyd happened only because he loved food, liked going to Floyd's restaurant in Bristol, put him on a local arts meets rock TV programme called *RPM*, and thought it would be fun to make a cookery series using the Stranglers' 'Peaches' as the soundtrack.

Why 'Peaches', I don't know, but it worked. There had been nothing like *Floyd on Fish* before, it was as if rock 'n' roll had met cookery. The truth is that David has remained the same ever since; he does what seems fun to him at the time and pursues it single-mindedly. Sometimes this can be a little disconcerting. He thinks it's funny that I am the clumsiest person on the planet and will go to enormous ends to film incidents of me tripping, banging, burning myself with hot fat, or cutting myself. Once when I sliced myself rather badly on a Japanese mandolin while making *Taste of the Sea*, he accused the cameraman, Julian Clinkard, of having no journalistic sense. Julian had stopped his camera as I was jumping up and down bleeding and swearing. David fumed that he could see it all coming and was just waiting to catch it on film. He calls me the 'talent' and says he's a 'mere technician', but I often feel that I'm just the material. However, a few years after the mandolin incident I was leaning over the stern of a massive trawler off the Scottish coast, doodling away on my long defunct Psion organizer, when suddenly he grabbed me and pulled me back over the deck as a ton net weight swung right through where my head had been seconds before. Maybe he does care after all.

The truth about David is that because he knows what he wants and has an uncanny ability to gauge what our audience wants too, working with him, though massively annoying at times, when he's overpoweringly in charge, is exhilarating because I always think we're onto something new. There is something reassuring about just letting things evolve when we are filming. Sure we have a schedule, but he takes delight in changing it all at the last minute because something, maybe a stall selling dried fish by the road we've just passed, has excited him. In a world where TV seems to have become more and more formulaic it's nice to have someone around with an eye for passing life. I'm not his best friend, Bernard is, but I'm very glad I'm his second best one.

Rick Stein
April 2009

PART I

PART I

A recipe for disaster

Once in a blue moon, when the tide and weather was right, I'd head out to sea. If you're thinking I'm a salty old sea dog – I'm not. The sea has to be flat, oily calm and the sun should have warmed it sufficiently so that it gives off an effervescence that tingles the nose with a whiff of old seaweed. It's the smell that transports me back to childhood and makes me want to take off my shirt and go paddling about in rock pools. I felt a bit guilty at first, but after a few times sneaking away from the office, those pinpricks of guilt changed to surges of pure joy.

I had a little boat, and a job in production and management at the BBC in Plymouth that I didn't care for very much. The production side, yes; management, no. So I'd clear off every so often, until the land was a misty haze behind me. Just in case there's a BBC employment lawyer reading this, I'd like to point out that I hadn't been properly introduced to the art, if that's what it is, of management. To me 'management' was saying 'hello and good morning' quite loudly to people I'd meet on the way to the office first thing. And it was a long time ago.

Someone *had* told me that the most important thing you can possibly do as a manager is to listen. So I did. But

3

I had noticed that people nearly always said the same thing at least three times when they came to see me for a chat, so I would find myself drifting off into luscious thoughts of fresh fish, garlic, and wine, or lamb chops, as I thought of what to have for dinner that night. Or I would think about fishing.

There is nothing quite as wonderful as skimming over a glassy sea with the warm, salty wind in your face and the prospect of catching lunch an hour or so away. Through the heat haze the villages of Kingsand and Cawsand with their pastel painted cottages looked as though they would be more at home on the Amalfi coast, but I used to think that I'd rather be here in Cornwall than Italy any day, because once the attraction of boating had worn off (and it does), you still had the wonderful early evening prospect of a foaming pint of bitter in the local pub, followed by roast beef with Yorkshire pudding (of course) and then *Inspector Morse* on TV.

I would take a mobile phone the size of a jerrycan (well it was 1984), just in case something really important came up, a bottle of cider and a Cornish pasty as a precaution in case lunch proved reluctant to take the bait. I'd fish for bass, but only ever caught mackerel. Many people regard mackerel as the second-hand Ford Fiesta of the fish world, but they are delicious straight out of the sea, dusted in seasoned flour and fried in butter, with just a smidgen of mustard and a splash of lemon juice – but I digress. As I usually do at the mention of food.

I used to tell my assistant that I was off on a research trip to meet up with a Mr Bass down in Cornwall. Sometimes the phone would ring and on rare occasions it would be John Shearer in Bristol. He was one of my bosses, and although he looked the spitting image of John Denver, many of my fellow producers in the BBC rather unfairly I think, called him Vlad, after the famous Transylvanian prince with a penchant for sticking large nails through the heads of anyone who caused him displeasure – but only when Mr Shearer was well out of earshot. I liked him, because he was so unswerving in his thoughts and didn't give a fig about tact and diplomacy. He made no secret of the fact that he thought the BBC was stuffed full of somewhat tired (and very often emotional) lacklustre staff who spent far too much time in the BBC Club.

For obvious reasons, his was the last voice I wanted to hear on a bright morning a mile off the Cornish coast, with the sun beating down and the waves gently lapping against the hull. I'd put on my serious voice, and speak quickly so he wouldn't be able to hear the seagulls mewing overhead, but on one occasion he became suspicious and asked me where I was. I thought of saying I was in a meeting, but I'd just pulled in six mackerel and they were wriggling and flapping at the bottom of the boat making a terrible din.

'Well John, since you asked, I'm actually at sea at the moment researching a possible series on fishing in the south-west. It's a very important industry down here, you know, and it's been largely ignored.'

Amazingly he told me he thought this was most commendable and wished other producers would get off their arses and get out there to find out what was really going on.

It was after one of these delightful fishing trips that I returned to the studio in Plymouth and was making my way to my office when I heard the strains of the Stranglers' classic song, 'Peaches'. The studio, with its imposing veranda, lawns, and rosebushes, reminded me of one of those convalescence homes you saw in black and white films about recuperating fighter pilots and torpedoed seamen that were so popular in the Fifties. I could easily imagine nurses in starched white summer uniforms wheeling the staff about in the lovely gardens and bringing them cups of tea. Appearances can often be misleading though, because in these sedate surroundings the likes of Angela Rippon, Sue Lawley, and Jill Dando started their illustrious broadcasting careers. Like any television station, no matter how small, it was full of talented people keen to progress in the industry, tempered with a sprinkling of those whose love affair with television had finished a long time ago and who were now longing for a caravan in Brittany. I wasn't quite sure where in this scenario I fitted in.

The sound of the Stranglers was coming from the technical area where they recorded and transferred programmes onto videotape. I had chosen this brilliant song to end a brand new series that I'd made, but was as yet unseen, called *Floyd on Fish*. I saw this as an antidote to all those rather starchy and clinical studio-based shows in which all the ingredients were measured out in teaspoons or carefully weighed, and they always had a finished dish they'd made earlier.

I'd never had so much fun making a television programme before and after long sunny days of filming, my ribs used to ache from laughing so much.

On one of the many screens in the room I could see that the end credits were running. They were superimposed over a shot of Keith Floyd, with a very young-looking Rick Stein, sitting down with full silver service on white linen, laid out on the deck of a trawler. It had all seemed like such a brilliant idea and I felt extremely pleased with myself as I entered the room. I didn't have a clue how all this technical stuff worked but I thought it would be quite interesting to see what my very first programme for BBC South West looked like on a real telly, rather than an editing machine.

'What a load of crap!' was the first utterance I heard coming from an open talkback (this is a microphone and speaker system, which lets people in the recording studio communicate with people in the control room).

Greg, the video operator, went to switch it off but as I was nearer to the speaker I stopped him.

'This is probably the worst programme ever to come out of Plymouth,' said another voice.

'That bloke's pissed out of his head. It's insulting.'

'It's a disgrace. It shouldn't be allowed,' said another.

Well I think there were a few more comments, but by then I felt as if my shiny brand new Spitfire was crashing down to earth with all my ammo used up and black smoke streaming from the engine cowling.

I could recognize nearly all of the voices. They belonged mostly to engineering staff, whom I'd see often in the BBC bar after work. Greg looked very embarrassed and kept finding interesting things to look at through the window. I put on one of my best smiles, the sort that says, 'Hey, am I worried? I really do appreciate these thoughts.

You've been most honest and I'll bear your criticisms in mind … When I come round to your house and set fire to it.'

I was smiling so much my face hurt but on the inside I was unsettled and a trifle scared. Maybe I had been too cavalier, too much under the spell of the mercurial Mr Floyd? All this time I'd been happily filming away at wonderful locations in the south-west without a care in the world. We'd eaten well, drunk rather too much, and probably in the process I'd created a false sense of euphoria. Now, I wondered to myself, if it really is as bad as they say, how could I possibly get something so wrong? I'd probably have to resign and become a freelance, or, worse, be faced with the sack. My mother would be horrified, not to mention my wife and daughter and the Bradford and Bingley. And this would mean no more expensive, over the top food shopping. Bye, bye Scottish sirloin and Gevrey Chambertin – not that I saw very much of you. Adieu roast goose washed down with a serious bottle of Pauillac – well that was only for birthdays really. Cheerio to all the lovely things I love so much, especially lobster, turbot and Iberico ham – although you were strictly for high days and holidays. I would be entering a bleak world where no doubt I'd have to beg a commissioning editor half my age to grant me the opportunity to make a film about the state of rural transport in north Devon.

The last time something like this had happened to me was in 1978, when I'd made a new series for the BBC in Bristol. It was called *RPM* and it was about pop music, architecture, real ale, and lots of other stuff – basically things that I and my small production team found interesting. It was new, it was vibrant – or so I thought – and it was due to run for thirteen weeks. I had high hopes for it.

A day or so after the first transmission they started to appear. 'They' were pinned on the notice board outside the canteen, up and down the corridors, outside the studios, everywhere. 'They' were cuttings from the *Bath Chronicle* and they carried a searing review of my very first programme. The headline in the television section screeched something like, 'Is this the worst television programme ever made by BBC Bristol?' Clearly someone who didn't care for the programme, or more likely, me, had been busy scampering around the studios with a roll of Sellotape.

Well, of course, I read the review – and then I read it again – desperately looking for something good that would stand out. I was searching for words like 'innovative' and 'brave', but the more I read it, the more I realized that the only good thing in there was the question mark. Something deep inside me told me not to touch these critiques that seemed to be everywhere; leave them where they were, and after a few weeks they'd shrivel up to brittle pieces of unreadable parchment, fall off and float away like autumn leaves, never to be seen again. As it happened *RPM* went on to be a big success and ran for eight years.

Over the years I had decided that there are four ingredients in the cocktail that is essential to the well-being of any television producer or director. One: an enquiring mind. Two (not surprisingly): imagination. Three: loads of passion. Four (and this was the big one): a total belief that whatever you do is going to be a resounding success. Optimism plays a large part in a director's bag of tricks. I've known directors waxing lyrical about the dullest of concepts. One of my friends spent over four years making a film about the construction of the Scottish Parliament building and he was as passionate about it as if he was making *Life on Earth*. I suppose in 400 years' time it might be quite interesting to see.

Also, I strongly believed in regional broadcasting, and still do, despite the fact that it has often been decimated over the last few years. I know that many executives and programme makers at the BBC in London think of the staff in the regions as rather like irritating sand fleas, but I see regional TV as a great place to experiment with new talent. *Floyd*, I thought, would never get off the ground in London. Most food programmes in those days came under the auspices of the Education Department and *Floyd* certainly wouldn't have made for a good proposal on paper. I could imagine a committee discussing the glasses of wine and the haranguing of the cameraman. I'm a great optimist, but I don't think they were quite ready for a culinary version of Reginald Bosanquet.

No, my plan was to make the programme with Floyd first and let the great and the good decide afterwards whether it worked or not. After all, as BBC features editor for the south-west, I was lucky enough to be my very own commissioning editor. So I didn't have to convince anyone, except myself, which was why, that afternoon, I was sitting on a train on the way to London, running scared.

The only thing to do in a situation like this, I had decided, was to consult someone whose opinion I really treasured. This could be a pretty risky strategy, but I was desperate, because I had already commissioned myself to make a further five programmes with Keith Floyd. I was on my way to seek the opinion of one of the most talented producers in the land at the time, my good friend and mentor, John Purdie. John made the award-winning fly on the wall series *Sailor*, filmed on the aircraft carrier HMS *Ark Royal*.

Armed with a video cassette and a bottle of champagne bought from an off-licence in Chelsea, I arrived at John's houseboat on the Thames. When he opened the door his little beady eyes lit up at the sight of the rather handsome bottle of Mumm. There are times when John reminds me of Captain Pugwash. He's even got a parrot.

In the snug sitting room on the barge I told John what I'd heard on the open talkback in the videotape room earlier in the day. I couldn't help but think that, for all our friendship, he was secretly enjoying my moment of intense insecurity. 'Schadenfreude', that lovely German word, is alive and well and thrives in the world of television. Although they pretend otherwise, television people love it when one of their friends makes an absolute turkey of a programme. After reading and savouring every ounce of vitriol in the newspaper reviews, they say things like, 'I haven't actually seen the programme but I've got it recorded and I've heard some good things about it. Is there anything in the papers?'

John covered the parrot's cage with a grey blanket. In my paranoia I thought it was because the parrot might leap from his perch and start stomping around the bottom of his cage shouting out what a load of crap my programme was, but I was assured it was only in order to have an uninterrupted viewing. I charged our glasses, lit a cigarette and waited while the video clock ticked its way to zero.

The opening titles saw our chef quaffing a glass of wine aboard various boats and fishing on the Somerset Levels, cooking and laughing his head off. All this joyous imagery was accompanied by the Stranglers anarchic 'Waltz in Black'. John watched unblinkingly, giving nothing away.

All television editors, directors and producers hate 'viewings', the tense affair when the commissioning editor or head of department casts their judgemental eye on a production that has inevitably taken months of blood, sweat and tears to create. Copious note-making by the boss is usually a serious sign of failure, spelling grim and uncertain times ahead for the producer and director.

I noticed that John had hardly touched his glass of champagne while I'd nearly finished the whole bottle, a most unusual state of affairs. But at least he wasn't making notes. Eventually, shortly after the scene where Keith Floyd says to the cameraman, 'Look, don't put the camera on me. Put it down there on the blinking scallops. Don't you understand, you idiot ... it's all about food? You simply can't get trained staff these days!' the screen went blank. John had switched the recording off. It was supposed to run for half an hour but after twelve minutes or so it seemed that my friend and mentor had had enough.

Peking duck heaven

I think it's worth a small gastronomic detour at this point to explain why John's opinion mattered so much.

I first worked with him in Hong Kong in 1976 making a series about the police called *The Hong Kong Beat*. He was a highly respected director and I was his researcher. Until then I hadn't been further than Lloret de Mar on a Club 18–30 holiday, so this hot and steamy colony in the South China Sea came as a bit of a shock – an extremely pleasant one. When we weren't in the back of police Land Rovers hoping for murder and mayhem (sadly I'm ashamed to say this is true) we would be in the street food markets that surrounded our hotel in Kowloon. I've been back to Hong Kong since and most of these street stalls have been swept away, but back then they were everywhere. For me they were the main attraction of the place, along with the Star Ferries which plied their way between Hong Kong Island and the mainland.

There was so much to choose from at the markets. Red ducks dripping with fat, and hunks of pork, the crackling cooked to golden perfection, hung from the frames of ramshackle counters. We'd normally be served by unsmiling, crew-cutted old men tossing a whole variety of vegetables and noodles in huge woks that, now and again, briefly caught fire. The stoves roared like jet engines, pushing out tremendous heat, so everything cooked quickly, which, of course, is the whole secret of this style of cooking; and the food was so cheap. Our mouths watered so much with anticipation that it became impossible to talk without spraying each other. This was the most delicious food I had ever tasted, and the combination of spicy noodles, crispy green vegetables, pork, duck, and prawns was light years away from any Chinese takeaway I'd ever had back home.

John was a true trencherman and like me had a ferocious appetite. Sometimes in the car driving back from filming in the New Territories, the country area by what was then the Chinese border, we would make up songs about how hungry we were. One day, John, in his soft Scottish burr told me about a restaurant he'd been to where the speciality was Peking duck. He described what he'd eaten: the soft pancakes smeared with plum sauce, the sweet crispy skin of the duck and the crunchy matchsticks of cucumber and spring onions. The way he described it, he had to take me to this restaurant now. Nothing else would do.

It was called the American Restaurant and it was everything John said it was. Although it was very early in the evening, the place was packed. Waiters wearing white gloves were carving huge golden brown ducks at the tables and the bamboo steamers they carried past us left a waft of sweet smelling dough in their wake. By the time a waiter came to take our order I was nearly passing out with hunger. John explained that we each wanted a duck and the full order of pancakes and the other accompaniments that go with it.

'No,' said the waiter, rather curtly I thought. 'You cannot have one duck each. You can only have one duck for two.'

John looked at him and explained we were both extremely hungry and that one duck would not be enough. Unfortunately this only made the waiter angry.

'One duck enough.'

He began to write the order down on his pad which upset my friend John enormously. 'He want duck,' he said, pointing to me, 'and I want duck.'

I nodded appreciatively and tried to give the impression that one duck to us would be no more than a mouthful.

It seemed we had reached an impasse and I was beginning to think that we were about to get unceremoniously chucked out of the best Peking duck restaurant in the world.

'Get me the manager,' said John.

'Why don't we just have one duck and share it?' I ventured helpfully. 'And if we're still hungry we could ask for another one.'

John gave me the kind of stare you get from the Scots when you unwittingly mistake them for Celtic instead of Rangers supporters and vice versa.

The manager arrived and was charm personified. He explained that the restaurant had been there since the war serving Peking duck and as far as he knew no one had ever ordered a duck each before. And so that evening John and I made history. They had to put another table next to ours to carve these enormous ducks which looked more like geese. I'm sure they found the two biggest birds in the kitchen to teach us a lesson. The waiters expertly separated the skin from the caramel coloured-flesh and left mountains of each before taking the carcasses away for the chefs to make soup.

'Make soup?' I said, looking at the piles of duck and the steamers full of pancakes.

'Yes,' said our grumpy waiter, but now he was smiling. 'First you have duck with pancakes and then you have duck soup. That's why one duck enough.'

Unfazed by this news, John showed me the art of making and rolling the perfect duck pancake: sauce first then a sprinklng of cucumber and spring onion, then equal portions of skin and meat, all rolled up like a cigar. Crunch. It was sweet and crispy with a lovely aftertaste of duck fat. Soon it became a race and by the time we had counted twenty pancakes each, a dogged silence prevailed. Over an hour later we were still eating. Our appetites had been sated long ago, but we both knew we must devour every morsel.

The pancakes finished, out came the bowls of soup, which were huge and challenging and eventually they beat us. However, the manager and the waiters seemed transformed and treated us with great civility when we eventually left the restaurant and wobbled out into the warm steamy night. Maybe, thirty years later, the staff still recount the story of the Englishman and the Scotsman who had one duck each but couldn't quite finish the soup.

So that is why the opinion of my friend was so important to me. Not only did John understand the world of television but food is his passion.

Now, I sat on his houseboat dreading his verdict. He turned to me and said rather gravely, 'We've just got enough time to buy another bottle of fizz before they close, because this is going to be a hit!'

Early next morning I caught the first train back to Plymouth and in four hours or so I was walking up the very same corridor that had seemed so gloomy yesterday. People were making their way to the canteen. I saw the usual faces grouped around their usual tables – engineers at one end of the room, journalists and features staff at the other. I recognized the four, or was it five, engineers who had painted such a bleak picture of my efforts. But that was yesterday. Such a very long time ago, and today I was happy and probably a little hung over from the night before. I was up in the world of sun-split clouds in my Spitfire again, the Merlin engine purring like a contented tiger, the wings full of ammo and down below me, clearly outlined against the silver sea, four, or was it five, Heinkel bombers, as fat as turkeys, were making their way home ... or so they thought. I pushed the stick forward and flipped the safety off.

'I think I'll have a nice cup of tea, Mrs Boggis, and one of your finest cheese scones, a nice warm one straight from the oven please.'

David believe me, cooking's the new rock 'n' roll

Floyd's Bistro in Bristol had a real touch of class. It was 1982, before the days of open-plan kitchens, white walls, washed wood, and chrome. Floyd's little restaurant smelt right, rather like those wonderful *cafés du commerce* that adorn any self-respecting market town in France. As soon as you opened the door you were greeted with a waft of good coffee, hot butter with a touch of garlic, and just a hint of Gauloise, Floyd's cigarette of choice. It even had a real grumpy French waiter, who looked like a consumptive Bryan Ferry. On one wall was a mounted head of a huge antelope or it might have been a gnu, its long horns festooned with hats and umbrellas. The Bistro was packed when we got there and we were shown to our table in the middle of the room.

I'd been tipped-off about Mr Floyd by Andy Batten-Foster, the presenter of *RPM*, which had been running for four years now. Andy had met Floyd before, in a Berni Inn, which might sound strange but there was nothing wrong with a Berni Inn in those days: a prawn cocktail, a decent steak, and black forest gateau, thank you. He really liked Keith and thought he'd be good to have on the programme. However, the thing that most impressed him was that a waitress had spilt a glass of red wine over the brand new Burberry trench coat that Floyd had bought that day and worn for the first time that evening. He was clearly proud of it because he didn't want to take it off. But he didn't bat an eyelid. Staring at the red stain he just said, 'Gracious me my dear, I wouldn't worry about that – all it needs is a damp cloth and it'll be fine.' But deep inside, Andy knew he was crying.

Andy had been talking to me for ages about Floyd's Bistro. Apparently he'd been once before when Floyd sent a table of four packing because they insisted on ordering well done steaks. In so many words Keith told his wide-eyed audience that his entrecôtes were of the finest quality, from pedigree cattle reared on lush Somerset meadows blessed with crystal streams and he was fucked if he was going to cook them well done thank you very much. He showed them the door and suggested if they hurry they might just make the Wimpy before it closed.

On another occasion a regular customer complained that his Wiener schnitzel, a thin escalope of veal dipped in egg and breadcrumbs, was really tough. Floyd came out of the kitchen, personally apologized to the man and took his plate away saying as he retreated that the most perfect Wiener schnitzel would be coming up any minute. Down in the kitchen Floyd was reputed to have cut a couple of beer mats roughly into the shape of schnitzels, soaked them in a little white wine to soften, rubbed them with garlic butter, seasoned them and dipped them in egg and breadcrumbs, and popped the lot into hot olive oil. The man ate it uncomplaining while Floyd, glass in hand, watched him joyously devour every mouthful. Such was the reputation of the man. Floyd offered a little bit of theatre in a rather staid part of Bristol. No wonder the place was packed.

On the night I went for dinner I can't remember who I was with but, such are my priorities, I do remember what I ate. We had clams followed by steak frites and a bottle of the house red. Because we were late arriving, it wasn't long before Keith made an appearance from his hot kitchen. He walked among the tables like an adjutant surveying the recruits' canteen, asking the occasional customer if everything was to their liking. He started chatting to an expensively dressed couple sitting at a table underneath the gnu or ibex or whatever it was. They had parked their new Porsche on the pavement outside and were spending much of their time admiring it. Without asking, Floyd helped himself to a large glass of their wine and then in a loud voice apologized for not having any scampi in the basket left because the Bristol Estate Agents Fine Dining Club had been in at lunchtime and scoffed the lot along with all the Blue Nun he had in the house. They thought this very funny and so did the rest of the diners. Who would he pick on next?

He reminded me of Graham Kerr of *Galloping Gourmet* fame. This was an imported series from New Zealand shown on the BBC in the early Seventies. Old ladies in the studio audience would be doubled up laughing as Mr Kerr leapt over chairs, simultaneously quaffing a glass of wine without spilling a drop. He'd gallop back to his kitchen area and fold in the béchamel sauce for the moussaka he was making. Then suddenly he'd dash off with a spoonful of seasoned minced lamb to another part of the studio and stuff it down the throat of some poor unsuspecting old dear. People weren't watching it because they wanted to learn how to cook, they were watching because the man was funny and having a good time – surely what entertainment and cooking are all about?

Well, of course, the inevitable happened. I think Floyd was saving us to last. After pouring himself a generous glass of our red wine, he started to tell us how much he disliked people who worked in television. As far as he was concerned they were all liars and cheats. 'They come into my restaurant pissed out of their heads, promising me the earth with my very own series. I break open my very best brandy, then they piss off and I never see them again.'

I couldn't help but notice he had eyes that one minute twinkled with merriment, and the next looked like they were on fire as if he was about to burst into tears, rather like a small boy who's had his fishing rod confiscated.

I told him I thought he was a very funny man who cooked well. I'm not sure whether he appreciated the word 'funny', but he went on to explain, in his sixty-a-day voice, how he had prepared the clams we'd had earlier. He talked passionately about his long love affair with Provence: the red wine, the olive oil, the fields of sunflowers and lavender, the soft golden light and the colour of the buildings, the spicy sausages and the salt cod with aioli. To him it was heaven and he yearned to get back there.

I think it was his voice that convinced me that he had something special about him. There was definitely a hint of danger about the man too. He reminded me of Richard Burton with a touch of Peter O'Toole. I wasn't quite sure whether he wanted to punch me in the face or pour me another glass of wine (sadly we'd run out). I said I'd really like him to make an appearance on *RPM*. My idea was for him to cook a main course for a dinner party for less than a pound a head. He told me to bugger off.

Undeterred, the next morning I drew up a little contract which included a small payment for him to appear on the programme and drove round to his restaurant. He opened the sash window upstairs, cigarette in hand, and I think he must have thought I was an over-enthusiastic customer, as he looked completely bemused.

I reminded him of our conversation the night before and said I'd be round the following day with a camera crew to film him creating a culinary masterpiece on a shoe-string.

When we arrived the next day there, on a crowded kitchen table, were four rabbits the size of whippets, bottles of Pouilly-Fumé, cognac, saffron, bunches of fresh purple garlic, large chunks of Bayonne ham, and a wicker basket full of apricot-coloured mushrooms. There must have been over a hundred pounds' worth of food in all, enough to feed at least twenty people, and I was paying for it.

So what happened to my wonderful idea of creating a meal for less than a pound a head? The short answer, as put by a slightly irritable Mr Floyd, was 'bollocks to that'. He told me he saw the filming as a God sent opportunity to show off his formidable culinary skills and to create a flavour of his beloved Provence. He thought my suggestion of cooking a dinner party menu for less than a pound a head quite tiresome and typical of some left-wing television producer who knew nothing about food. (He called me left wing. I felt quite proud. I'd never been called that before.) I should have seen the warning signs then.

That was how our first filming session started. The rabbit dish was superb and there was loads left over. Was there rabbit with wild mushrooms, simmered gently in white wine, on the menu that night at Floyd's Bistro for a modest twelve pounds or so? I wonder. The filming wasn't terribly good, but Floyd did say one thing that day I'll never forget – that cooking was the new rock 'n' roll.

'Cooks on television,' he pronounced, 'could be as famous as rock musicians and racing car drivers.'

I didn't believe him at the time, but I do now.

Twenty-five years ago no one could have foreseen the incredible popularity commanded by food programmes on television today. Now we have a whole army of chefs representing virtually every personality trait. Sexy, aggressive, posh, young, practical, not so young, pioneering, grumpy, scientific, philosophical, funny – and then, of course, Delia.

In the late Seventies and early Eighties there were many programmes about food and cookery on television but they were mostly huddled together on BBC2. Fanny Cradock and her poor downtrodden husband Johnny, along with her young traumatized assistants, were on our screens for years doing mind-boggling things with coloured piped mashed potato. I found it impossible to think of her as a happy fulfilled woman. She looked as if she'd spent the night crying her heart out and had hurriedly and, not too expertly, applied some extra make-up before walking into the studio. I watched her not so much for the culinary tips, but because I liked seeing her berate her monocle-wearing husband for getting in the way.

Then there were the mellifluous tones of the highly respected Derek Cooper introducing the viewers to his world of cooking. Marguerite Patten popped up from time to time. I regard her as the matriarch of all television cooking shows. Madhur Jaffrey hit the gastronomic bull's eye by teaching us how to make a proper curry using fenugreek and tamarind. Ken Hom did more for the wok-making industry than Chairman Mao and the exotic Robert Carrier taught us about tagines and couscous from his home in Morocco. Glynn Christian, a direct descendant of the famous Fletcher who cut the intolerant Captain Bligh adrift in the South Seas, entertained us for a while before drifting off himself somewhere I know not where. It was a pretty crowded house but through it all Delia's star got brighter and brighter. And years later, even when she boiled an egg, over three million people tuned in to see it wobbling around in a saucepan of simmering water – hoping, no doubt, it would be as hard as rock when she cracked it open. Like many a male viewer I found her quite sexy, but a bit schoolmarmish (maybe that was the attraction), and her food looked appetizing. Clearly she was someone the viewer could trust, like the sensible girl next door who does shopping for elderly neighbours. Inexplicably I had an overriding sensation that she was standing on casters and being pulled around the television studio on a long piece of string by a member of the production team, and that as soon as she stopped filming she'd crack open a bottle of white, open up the Silk Cut and put on Led Zeppelin.

There were so many cooking programmes in the early Eighties that journalists started to get quite cross about them. 'Not another one!' they would cry. 'Surely enough's enough?'

But Floyd was different. Until then, cookery on television was really aimed at women. When Floyd came on to our screens he gave men a clear and open invitation to get into the kitchen and have a go for themselves. Forget about exact ingredients, pour yourself a glass of wine and relax. Peel a couple of cloves of garlic and make the whole cooking experience far more enjoyable than going out to a restaurant.

Floyd made it OK for blokes in pubs to have conversations about chillies and coriander, and what's more, he cut down the fences that surrounded this relatively safe field of TV cookery shows, letting in what was to build up into a stampede of new, strange, and sometimes dangerous animals. Now cookery shows have spilt over from BBC2 onto Channel 4 and ITV where a healthy dollop of testosterone and foul language make them 'showbiz'. Add to that a smidgen of threatened violence, and it becomes almost gladiatorial. The boundaries are being shifted every few weeks with the likes of Hugh Fearnley-Whittingstall and Jamie Oliver highlighting the unsavoury practices of factory farming and alerting the nation to an epidemic of fat schoolchildren. These TV chefs have become more effective and powerful than a roomful of MPs, and I'm talking about a pretty big room here.

I read somewhere that the excellent Anthony Worrall Thompson said that we all got our TV careers because of Floyd. I know that it was Keith Floyd who inspired a very young Jamie Oliver to be a chef. Floyd was right. Cooks have become as famous as racing drivers and rock musicians, probably even more so.

But none of this had happened yet. The programme with Floyd and his very expensive rabbit dish was shown on *RPM* sandwiched between a Stranglers' concert and a Sixties guide to the West Country presented by that wonderful writer and broadcaster Ray Gosling; a world of Teddy Boys, street parties, frothy coffee, mini skirts, skiffle and scooters, interspersed with a host of curious and quirky items from the BBC's treasure trove of old news films. It would be an understatement to say Floyd didn't fit in terribly well, and many people told me so, including my boss.

'What on earth has that idiot cooking a rabbit got to do with the programme?' he asked.

I thought about it for some time, but I couldn't really come up with an answer. It was nearly a year before I was to meet up with Floyd again.

In the meantime, I went off around Britain with that eccentric Liverpudlian Beryl Bainbridge, following in the footsteps of J. B. Priestley's *English Journey*. I learnt a lot from her; not least how to drink large 'Rusty Nails', a mixture of whisky and Drambuie.

There was a memorable moment when we arrived in her home town and she led us down a street where the houses were all boarded up, ready for demolition. She looked up at one of them and said, 'David, that's where I was brought up.'

We had to film this poignant moment, I thought. So we pulled the corrugated iron off one of the windows and climbed into this scene of devastation. There were daubings on the wall and unmentionable things on the floor; some of the boards had been ripped up to make a fire. I could see she was moved to tears as we walked through the house, through the front room where, she said, her mum and dad used to argue, while she would be upstairs listening. We climbed the stairs, looked into her bedroom, and her eyes were welling up. She lit several cigarettes and stared wistfully out at the backyard, all tumbled down and covered in stinging nettles and overgrown weeds. Eventually we climbed out of the window and she stood there looking back at the house. I found the whole thing terribly moving, and I told her so.

Then she turned to me and said, 'David, it wasn't that house. It was the one next door.'

The owl and the pussy cat went to sea – eventually

From time to time at the BBC you were encouraged to apply for another job. I think it was a measure adopted by large organizations to avoid complacency. Jimmy Dewar, my irascible and generous boss in Bristol, thought it the most sensible thing to do.

'Look at it this way,' he said, pouring me a large gin and tonic. 'You'll be seen as someone who wants to get on in life and to develop other skills. And, anyway, there are quite a few applicants for the Plymouth job so the chances are that you won't get it.'

'What if I do get it and say I've had a change of heart?' He gave me one of those looks that Captain Mainwaring usually reserves for Private Pike.

It was a bit of a shock leaving Bristol to move to Plymouth and take up my new job as features editor there. I remember Alan Clark, the diarist and MP, saying the best view of Plymouth was in the rear-view mirror of his Porsche as he went hell for leather back home to Kent. The centre of the city is improving now and promises to be a mini version of Barcelona in five years' time – both cities have the sea in common – but back in the early Eighties it was depressing. The city centre, apart from a couple of large department stores, was a pedestrianized zone of cheap low-rise buildings, the result during the last war of the Luftwaffe bombing every structure that had some architectural merit. While it had been uplifting to spend a lunch hour in Bristol, walking down the lovely Park Street, here all I saw were swathes of people dawdling along the pavements, dressed in tracksuits and munching on Cornish pasties from paper bags.

The best bit of Plymouth by far was the Barbican, and the best bit of the Barbican was the fish market, right next to the old harbour where the *Mayflower* sailed to the New World. Plymouth has a new, much smarter fish market these days, where members of the public are not particularly welcome, which is an enormous pity, but in the early Eighties Brussels and all its Health and Safety brigades hadn't put Plymouth on its list of things to do. Most of the fish merchants had cigarettes stuck in the corners of their mouths as they slid their filleting knives swiftly over the framework of bones.

Hogarth and his sketchbook wouldn't have looked too out of place in the old fish market. I'd very often see a man inspecting the fish, dressed like Sir Francis Drake in doublet and hose, with a well-trimmed beard and a natty little hat. He looked quite at home among the glistening cobblestones. Apparently he would take groups of schoolchildren around the narrow streets that led down to the harbour and he'd bring to life those days of the Armada, pox, and rum. Occasionally I'd see him in Sainsbury's with his flashy rings and buckles and a large cutlass swinging from his hip. It was an odd sight to see such a figure reading the small print on a pot of yoghurt.

I loved that fish market, awash with water and ice and disdainful looking seagulls strutting around the fish boxes looking for a tasty morsel. In the winter I'd buy the finest lemon soles for supper. They were firm and thick and landed just a few hours before and they smelt sweetly of the sea itself. In the summer I'd buy turbot and red mullet and it was on one of those fish-buying trips that the proverbial light bulb went on and completely changed my life for ever.

The fish merchants were true artists of the knife, leaving not a scintilla of wasted flesh behind as they filleted their fish; but they tended to be grumpy until they got to know you. One day when I was shopping there, Fred Brimmacombe, a fish merchant who wore a sailor's hat with so many badges on it you could hardly see the cloth, was having a bit of a rant.

'All people in this country want is cod, plaice and 'addock.' He started to point with his razor-sharp filleting knife. 'All these red mullet, all these cuttlefish, these 'ere gurnards, is all shipped over to Spain.' Fred was getting a bit cross now, walking across the slippery fish boxes, balancing on their edges like an angry seal. 'The mentality over 'ere is, if we don't bloody well know what these fish are, we don't bloody eat 'em. It's a bloody shame. It breaks my 'eart it does, to see all this good fish sent over there to arrive three or four days later in some bloody Spanish port, way past its prime. It's a national disgrace it is. It really bloody is.'

What an interesting subject, I thought. Here we had all these lovely fish arriving as fresh as daisies and we were selling them to the Spanish and also the French because we didn't fancy eating them ourselves. Could it be that as an island we were a bunch of fish haters because in days past fish was just too plentiful? I could remember when I came home from school and the house used to stink of fish because my mother boiled cod shoulders for the cat's tea. It put me off fish for years.

But thanks to Fred Brimmacombe, I knew what my new programme was going to be about. It was going to be an evangelical food programme led by my very own Billy Graham, the man I'd met many months earlier in a Bristol restaurant. I could see Keith Floyd as the fishermen's champion, showing the people at home how silly it was to export all this fresh, cheap fish to the Continent when we should be eating it ourselves. And this wouldn't be a five-minute flash in the pan wedged between a rock band and a film on the architecture of Swindon. This would be a whole programme devoted to this dreadful waste of a precious resource. It might even be a series.

Maybe I should nip up to Bristol now to see Keith for a drink and start making plans, I thought. But the turbot looked far too good. I imagined it gently poached in a court bouillon for fifteen minutes or so and then served with hollandaise, new potatoes, and watercress. Maybe I'd see him tomorrow.

When we met again Floyd had lost a bit of his sparkle. He was in the kitchen of his bistro on the phone and having a difficult time judging by the way he was dragging on his cigarette. I gathered from the bits of conversation I was trying not to hear that he was immersed in financial difficulties, and from what I could glean, the person on the other end of the phone was refusing to deliver any more produce until the bill was settled. It was a painful telephone call which had gone well beyond that old familiar stopgap of 'a cheque is in the post'. I wished I had arrived a bit later because he looked completely dejected as he put the receiver down, and not at all like the swaggering adjutant I'd seen all those months before.

He was in the middle of cooking freshwater crayfish and I'd never set eyes on one before. What beautifully designed things they were, rather like cherry-red Match-box edition toy lobsters crossed with JCBs. They were being extremely aggressive to each other and I could imagine that if they were the size of dachshunds they'd take over the world. I discovered over lunch they also tasted wonderful, like sweet nutty shrimps. Floyd didn't eat very much. He was drinking large Scotches with lots of ice and puffing away on endless cigarettes, detailing his thoughts on why the British people have no respect for good food, while the French revere it.

I toyed with the idea of contradicting him by pointing to the hillock of discarded crayfish shells on my plate, compared to his rather full ashtray, but thought it best not to. It dawned on me at the time that one of the differences between a gourmand and a gourmet might well be this: a gourmet is someone with a relatively small appetite and an academic interest in food, who'd rather talk about it than eat it; a gourmand relishes the infinite joys and pleasures of eating.

During lunch we discussed filming, money, locations, dishes. In fact, the money was a bit of a sticking point because everyone at that time assumed television had money to burn, after all it was seen as a glamorous industry. But regional television, along with local radio, was the church mouse of the BBC and the budgets reflected that. Two thousand pounds was all I had to make each half-hour programme of *Floyd on Fish*, a programme destined to be shown in the south-west only. This meagre budget had to pay for Keith, the film crew, travel and accommodation, film stock and hospitality, which inevitably included many bottles of wine. My salary and the post production costs like editing and dubbing were excluded from that sum. This was 1984. To make a similar programme today you'd have to multiply that figure by twenty-five at least.

Am I supposed to rehearse this? And do I need more than one fish?

I used to have a recurring nightmare while learning the rudiments of rugby at school. I found the rules of rugby union extremely complicated, especially things like the offside regulation, and the fact that you had to pass the ball backwards to your teammates seemed totally unnatural. It seemed to me the game would be so much more interesting if you were allowed to throw the ball forwards. And as for scrums; what on earth was that all about? In my nightmare I would find myself playing for the England Colts at Twickenham, with the stands packed with young enthusiasts. I'd be fortunate enough to catch a high pass but would find myself stopping for a few moments to decide what to do. Should I run with the ball? Should I pass it back or kick it forward? In the meantime a whole mountain of flesh from the opposing side would fall on me and afterwards the scorn of the crowd and fellow members of my team would sound like 10,000 baying wolves. 'Look,' I would say, standing alone on the pitch, 'this is very complicated. I was just trying to decide what was the best thing to do.' Such was my quandary now.

Our very first location was at a fine restaurant in Devon called the Horn of Plenty and it was run by Sonia Stevenson, a lively woman with a cut-glass accent and a deep passion for food. She said she first wanted to be a cook when she started to make mud pies with her friends as a child. An assistant producer at Plymouth, Jeremy Mills, suggested we shoot there because of her formidable reputation as a cook.

Floyd and I drove through the high hedgerows of Devon to the restaurant. Bluebells, red campions and primroses lined the way as we crunched over the gravel that led to the entrance of this imposing Victorian house. Sonia was waiting on the front steps dressed in her chef's whites and looking very professional. Warming to the theme of our programme, she said she had chosen to cook hake in a lemon and butter sauce because the Spanish were nicking all these lovely fish from around our coasts and she wanted to show people how good they were. Splendid, said Floyd, rubbing his hands together.

We started to film and suddenly I realized why, until now, all those cookery shows had been recorded in a studio. With four cameras or so you can have a whole assortment of shots, from close-ups of the ingredients to a wide angle of the kitchen, as well as mid-shots of the cook and guest. But where was my *one* camera supposed to be looking? At Floyd's face? At his hands? In the cooking pot? Where? The film was rolling through and I kept it on a shot wide enough to see Keith and Sonia plus the fish and the other ingredients. I think I had a touch of 'rabbit in the headlights' syndrome.

Apart from making a very short item with Floyd cooking his rabbit dish, I'd never done anything like this before. Fortunately I was saved by the cameraman, Malcolm Baldwin, suggesting that it would be quite a good idea to cut at this point and set up a closer shot of the subject, which was the fish. 'Ah! I get it,' I thought, as Sonia started to cut the hake into cutlets – but what happens next? It was a bit like a jigsaw puzzle, except you had to saw out the pieces personally before you began.

Day one of a new series, and technically I wasn't up to it: it was a pretty cathartic moment for me. I could tell by the way Floyd was looking at me that he knew I'd lost the plot. I could feel the respect levels plummeting and I thought to myself, 'I wish I hadn't done this. *I wish I hadn't done this.*' A director has to be in charge, or everything spirals out of control.

I learnt a set of valuable lessons that day and they are: do a thorough 'recce' of the location; discuss in detail the actual cooking process, something you should be able to commit to memory; and make sure there's another stand-in fish and duplicate ingredients so that you can film all the close-ups of the cooking process in beautiful back-lit photography later on. Also, if the camera is stuck on a tripod, there is very little it can do, whereas if it is hand-held it becomes the viewer's eager eye. I just wish some-one had told me before. It would have saved so much pain and angst.

Old dogs *can* learn new tricks

Very early in morning after filming at The Horn of Plenty, Keith, me and the crew were on a trawler head-ing out of Plymouth Sound on our way to the fishing grounds about twenty miles out. I've been on many trawlers since and regardless of nationality and age they all seem to smell the same: cigarette smoke, diesel, and a whiff of last week's fish. There was one more important lesson I had learnt by the end of yesterday's filming, and that was: as the programme was called *Floyd on Fish*, it should be Keith doing the cooking, not anyone else, because that's what I hired him for in the first place. So after filming with Sonia we had visited The Navy, a pub on Plymouth's Barbican, and held a council of war.

'When they bring up the net,' I said to Keith, 'why don't you select a lovely fish and cook it on-board for the trawler crew?' There was a long silence as people thought it over.

'Let's get this right,' said Floyd, pulling on his cigarette. 'You want me to cook on a trawler. We don't even know if it has a galley to cook in, let alone any implements.'

That's true, I thought, but surely they all have galleys because sometimes they're out there for days, if not a week at a time, and their sandwiches would get mighty stale and curly if they didn't.

After a while, rather like the doctor in a cowboy film instructing the gunslinger who has to help him deliver a baby in the wilds of Arizona, Floyd said, 'OK! I'll need some cream, a skillet, a sharp knife, a spatula, butter, cider, parsley and chives, and you'd better bring a camping stove just in case.'

Now, out in the English Channel on a trawler swaying from side to side in a force-five wind, we waited patiently before we heard the clank of chains and the whine of the winch which signalled the net was about to come aboard. Suddenly, from nowhere, there were dozens of seagulls screeching overhead. This was a really exciting moment because no one knew what the net would contain. It took an age to bring it in and then it was hoisted on a jib above the deck like a giant haggis, swaying and spraying water and smelling of the very essence of the sea. The skipper gave the order to release the cod end – that's the knot at the bottom of the net – and out spilt a bizarre collection of fish, seaweed, rocks, lots of mud and bits of old motorbikes. Then a hose was turned onto this muddy heap and you could start to see the beautiful fish shining like jewels: hake, scallop shells, a couple of ling, whiting, and pollack and there, in the middle, as ugly as sin, a monkfish.

In the tiny galley barely big enough for two people Floyd was on top form, cooking his monkfish the way they do in Normandy. It didn't take very long and in a way he began to take over the directing of the scene himself by suggesting to the camera that it would be jolly nice to see the cream go in on a close-up shot so that people could watch it amalgamate with the cider. I couldn't help notice the faces of the skipper and deck-hand as they peered through the window at him from the wheelhouse; they must have thought we were all barking mad. I had to keep my eyes firmly on the horizon, desperately fighting a losing battle against the relentless tide of nausea sweeping over me, as Floyd served the fish up on a plate that had seen better days, and with a couple of forks he found in a drawer, offered it up to the crew to try. It looked good, as good as if it had been prepared in a restaurant in Honfleur. The fish was firm and white and the cider sauce was a velvety pale gold, flecked with green from the herbs. After sampling a mouthful, the fisher-men said they liked it, but being fishermen they didn't enthuse too much. Curiously, it was the first time either of them had tasted monkfish. I had the distinct feeling they would have much preferred a bacon sandwich.

The next day we found ourselves filming in Newlyn fish market. Markets are a joy to film in, because as a general rule fishermen and fish merchants don't give a tinker's cuss about being filmed and just get on with the business of making money. There's a lot of noise and bustle and men with beards and beer bellies who do, however, have a slightly menacing attitude towards incomers. Making a living from the sea is a hard life and if you don't belong to the fraternity then you don't really belong here. I think we all sensed this while we were nursing our hangovers and desperately trying to avoid being run over by forklift trucks.

I don't think it helped that Floyd was wearing a very expensive Burberry trench coat and a brown trilby hat. He looked as if he'd be more at home at Goodwood or Newmarket. We filmed Keith wandering around the boxes of fish, stopping occasionally to pick up a good specimen and put it down, and oddly I noticed that wherever he went he left a trail of fishermen in his wake doubled up with laughter. I knew he was charismatic, but this was extraordinary. These men were normally dour and suspicious, but here they were laughing at whatever Keith was saying (which I couldn't hear because I didn't have headphones on). Then I realized what had caused such mirth. Someone had stuck a label on the back of his expensive raincoat saying 'fresh prick'.

I could hardly breathe for laughing so much but Floyd really didn't find it funny at all. In fact, he looked quite hurt. When I'd finally stopped laughing I suggested that Keith should tell the audience what kind of unusual fish there were in the market that morning, preferably fish the merchants couldn't sell in England and were shipping off to Spain and France instead. I should have known that Keith hates to be made a fool of and will always try to get his own back in any way he can.

Once the camera was rolling he picked up a red mullet and said what wonderful fish these were; in France they were highly revered and they called them the woodcock of the sea, because like woodcock, they were cooked with their guts intact. He then went on to talk about other fish that we as a nation ignore, preferring the safer options of cod, plaice, and haddock. Finally he took a fish I'd never seen before. It was a handsome browny-green fish with a spiky, lethal-looking dorsal fin.

'And now my little gastronauts,' said Floyd to the camera – and I may not have this word perfect, but it went something like this – 'I want to tell you about this chap here. He's called a weaver and over in France they serve him in bouillabaisse. He's got a wonderful sweet flavour and a firm texture but over here he's regarded as a nuisance because people might tread on him and have to be carted off to hospital.'

He then went on to suggest that the camera show a close-up of the spines of the weaver fish. 'Look at these *pricks*,' he said (rising emphasis on the word pricks I noticed), 'because they could do you serious harm – and there seem to be an awful lot of pricks in this fish market.' Point taken.

That evening Floyd visited a tarot card reader. He didn't have to go very far because she was sitting near the entrance to the restaurant where we were eating with the crew. I couldn't hear what she was saying but I could tell that she fancied him and it looked as if the feeling was mutual. They were drinking wine and laughing, and occasionally glancing back at the table where I was sitting with the crew. Eventually the consultation ended and he returned to his seat. With a beaming grin he told us the cards could foresee a tremendous future for him. He would become a household name and all his money worries would be a thing of the past. However, before he reached the heights of his powers the relationship with the 'joker' (I assumed he meant me) would be too strained to continue and would cease. Bloody hell, I thought, 'we haven't made one programme yet and already I have a sense of doom'. It took a few years, but the tarot reader was right.

Fair stood the wind for France

Halfway through filming our first series, *Floyd on Fish*, we caught the ferry to Saint-Malo. The idea was to test that old fish merchant Fred Brimmacombe's theory that the French adore practically anything that comes from the sea whereas we, with a few exceptions, prefer cod, plaice, and haddock.

Just a hundred miles south of Plymouth there's a whole different attitude to the fishy delights that come from this piece of sea separating our two countries. The thing that interested me was why that should be. Was it history or circumstance, maybe due to hardship or war?

When I first set eyes on the town from the deck of the ferry I thought how beautiful it looked, like a huge Walt Disney castle with mighty walls and towers and turrets rising from the sea. Conversely, I thought of the first thing that would greet passengers when they sail from

France to Plymouth – a large, smouldering scrap metal yard right next to the docks. I felt sure, after seeing this delightful town from the ship, we'd find people eating small hillocks of shellfish on every street corner and I wasn't wrong.

We were here for three days, enough time to film the fish market in the morning, maybe a restaurant at lunchtime and possibly the famous oyster beds in the afternoon. After leaving our kit at the hotel it was time to get our bearings and begin to explore the town. It was late afternoon now and beginning to get cold. The all important fish market was empty at this hour, the stone counters washed down ready for business the next morning. We walked through the narrow ancient streets with their high walls. It was like a film set in which you might turn a corner and glimpse a weary knight returning from the Crusades, leading his trusty steed in search of lodgings for the night. Just six hours on a ferry and we had arrived in a different world.

After a couple of drinks we thought we'd find somewhere in which to eat all sorts of fish for the entire evening. Floyd announced, 'I'll find a really good restaurant but you've got to trust me. I don't want to read any guides, I'll just do it by sight, smell, and gut instinct.'

He examined the menu of the first restaurant, built into the town wall by the main entrance. We waited patiently while he had a peep inside, before declaring it far too expensive, but perfect for Americans who didn't know any better. We continued, like a band of hunters, with Keith as our German pointer flushing out pheasants. He'd pop into a hotel and come out a few seconds later only to give it the thumbs down. There were six of us, including Clive the cameraman, Timmy on sound, Andy, the assistant cameraman, who also helped with the lights, and Frances Wallis, my trusty Scottish assistant and mother to us all – and we were all ravenous. I was dreaming of half a dozen oysters, followed by fish soup and maybe a large grilled Dover sole and a bottle of fresh, clean-tasting Muscadet, but still we traipsed on. Fortunately Saint-Malo is a compact town.

Finally, Keith stopped outside a small place with steamed-up windows called Au Gai Bec (At the Happy Mouth).

'This is what I was looking for,' he said. A warm glow, the sound of good conversation and clinking plates were coming from inside. 'You can keep your Michelin stars. Steamed-up windows: the first sign of a busy, happy restaurant.'

We went in and the warmth and smells of buttery fish soup, garlic, and a hint of Gauloise hit us straight away. Curiously it wasn't dissimilar to Keith's Bistro back in Bristol. It was packed, but the owner, who wore Buddy Holly glasses, asked us to wait and have a drink at the small bar. From where we were standing you could glimpse the kitchen where a young woman and an older lady – her mother perhaps – toiled over an antiquated stove. It was perfect.

That evening was one of the happiest we ever spent as a film crew on the road. The food was quite wonderful. We shared a large platter of fruits de mer, like a glossary of seafood from the continental shelf: oysters and shrimps, clams of every size, winkles and whelks and raw

cockles. Next we had a freshly made *cotriade*, a Breton
fish stew made with that day's catch, which included
meaty chunks of conger eel, mackerel, and sardines. We
were the last customers in the place, a perfect opportunity to get to know the owner, Jacques Yves. We didn't
need to tell him how much we enjoyed the food, but we
did anyway. Over a fine pear tart and sorbets made with
Calvados we told him of our mission to understand
France's love affair with fish. He assured us that we'd
come to the right place and promised to help us in any
way he could. In true Field Marshal Montgomery fashion we declared that from that moment on the Happy
Mouth would be our brigade headquarters – and it was,
for a number of years to come.

The next day involved a very early start and already, in
that lovely restaurant where we were so happy, it had gone
past midnight. Jacques Yves said that to wind down he
usually had a nightcap on his way home, in a little bar
not far away from here.

'No, no,' I protested. 'It's important we all get a good
night's sleep because we have to film in the fish market
at first light and that is the sole (no pun intended) reason
we came here in the first place. So let's have no more talk
of nightcaps. It's bedtime now and that includes everybody.'

Approximately two hours later Keith and I tottered
back along the cobbled streets to our hotel, feeling
extremely happy with ourselves. Of course, Clive, Timmy,
Andy, and Frances had sensibly gone to bed as soon as the
meal was over and Keith and I had only popped in out
of politeness really, but Jacques Yves was quite right, it

was a lovely little bar, and once the locals found we were from the BBC they wouldn't let us buy a drink.

The next morning I had a hangover of humungous proportions and worse, far worse, I'd slept through my alarm call. Even the hotel manager hadn't been able to wake me. And so the others all went off to film at the market while I slept on. It was an unforgivable act and I was deeply ashamed. In times of war I'd have been tied to a cannon wheel and shot – deservedly so. However, as luck would have it, there weren't too many locals out buying fish that early in the morning. Apparently, the market wouldn't start to get busy until ten o'clock when the sun had crept over the high walls of the town, flooding the streets with golden light. So Keith and the crew had returned to the hotel for café au lait served in huge ceramic bowls and warm, fresh croissants with apricot jam. Thank you God.

When we returned to the market the stallholders seemed much less grumpy than their British counterparts. Maybe it was because they were so busy. There were rows and rows of tables piled high with oysters, all neatly marked in order of size. In my limited experience I knew the smaller native oysters – the flat ones with smooth shells – to be by far the best tasting. Then there were heaps of lively pink and apricot-coloured langoustines, clearly landed that morning, judging by the way they were trying to walk out of the market. The langoustine should be the culinary symbol of Brittany. Here the locals eat them simply boiled and served with mayonnaise. I made a note we had to try some before catching the ferry the next morning.

44

There was a large cauldron of whelks being boiled in seawater then scooped up with a huge wire ladle and unceremoniously plonked into fish boxes. I knew my hangover was fading fast when that hot shellfish aroma from the whelks, reminiscent of freshly cooked lobster, started to make me think about lunch.

Keith was on top form in the market and knew all the names of the fish on display and how best to cook them. We discovered that most of the brown crabs had come from Cornwall and Devon, and that fishing boats from Plymouth very often called in to land their catch. I'm not sure if it was strictly legal, but it made sound sense if you'd just caught a boatful of red mullet and John Dory in the middle of the English Channel. The prices would be a lot better than at home because the locals love eating fish like these. I wouldn't mind betting it was the sort of trade that had secretly been going on since long before the Napoleonic Wars.

After an hour or so we'd filmed everything we needed and I thought it would be a good idea to visit the famous oyster beds in Cancale, a short drive away to the east. I was expecting something quaint and pretty, perhaps a few ancient thatched cottages huddled alongside a creek, where gnarled old men toiled in sailing boats dredging up oysters. So I was a bit taken aback by the sight of miles and miles of flat muddy shoreline, covered, as far as the eye could see, with black sacks. On closer inspection the sacks were made out of plastic mesh and were full of baby oysters the size of thumbnails. The mesh ensured that the sea would give them the precious nutrients they needed to grow, and the sack gave them protection from seabirds and stopped them from being swept away. The tiny oysters looked like so many pieces of chipped stone, but such was their reputation that in four years or so they could be gracing the tables of the Ritz and the Savoy.

It was a scene reminiscent of an L. S. Lowry painting, dotted with matchstick figures, some of them with rakes, some driving tractors, and others bent double, sewing up sacks. There were little paths made of concrete that wove their way along the beach and down to the shoreline. In the distance we spotted a line of schoolchildren following their teacher. At first we thought, 'What on earth are children doing in the middle of this muddy beach on a school day?' And then we realized this was why the French are so appreciative about food; they learn about it from an early age. We traipsed along the beach with the camera equipment and sure enough the teacher told us that this group of eight-year-olds would, as part of their education, visit farms, cheese-makers, and other local producers to learn about food, where it comes from and how it is grown and reared. I thought of the children at home who thought that milk came out of bottles and fish really did have fingers.

Over here, Clive

On our return from France something happened in Bridport that changed things for ever. It was here that Floyd found the person he really wanted to be on television; the persona that the technicians at Plymouth had pronounced crap, and that John Purdie had predicted was destined for stardom.

During the morning we'd been filming the scallop boats returning to the narrow harbour at West Bay. Nowadays this part of the Dorset coast is famous for its hand-dived scallops. Divers wearing aqualungs scour the seabed looking for scallops of the right size. It's a great way to preserve the stock; as with line-caught fish you take what you need and leave the rest for another day. All those years ago this method of fishing was just starting in Lyme Bay, but most of the local scallop fishermen still used small trawlers to dredge for them. Someone said it was a bit like using a tractor to weed an ornamental flowerbed. The trawler scooped up everything that came before it and its heavy chains could sometimes break the shells of the scallops. It was a couple of hours or so before each dredge was brought to the surface, which meant the shellfish, along with the rocks and mud and all the rubbish from the seabed, were tossed around as if they were in some infernal washing machine.

That afternoon we had planned to film Keith cooking king scallops in a pub, The George, in the centre of Bridport, which was very popular because they served really good coffee, freshly squeezed orange juice, and fabulous steak and chips. The problem was they were so busy we couldn't get into the kitchen because the staff were still bustling around preparing lunches. We would have to wait, so maybe it would be a good idea to have a pint or a glass of wine or two.

Julie, Keith's wife, had joined us, keen to see how her husband was coping in his new role as a television chef.

She looked perturbed when another bottle of wine turned up, but when it came time to film, Keith seemed on sparkling form, having had just the right amount of alcohol to soothe his nerves and sharpen his wits – a delicate balancing act. He began by opening the scallops and cleaning them and went on to sauté them in butter with wine, garlic and parsley.

Then, in a seminal moment he said to the cameraman, 'Why are you looking at me when you should be looking in the pot?' Like an obedient dog the camera went jerkily over to the pan where the scallops were frying gently. 'Look,' he commanded. 'Back over to me, if you please.' The camera creakily returned to its original shot and Floyd announced, 'I'm not a cameraman, I'm not a director. I know nothing about making television programmes, because I'm a cook. What I do know, however, is the star of the show isn't me. It's the food. So go back on to the pot and don't come up again until I tell you to!'

Julie was looking anxious. As soon as we'd finished filming she came over to me. 'David,' she asked. 'Please don't leave that bit about the camera in. It makes him look so drunk and arrogant.'

But for me Keith's outburst was a turning point that set a style for the programme for years to come. It was funny, engaging, and different, like one of those moments in a play when the actor tells the audience what they really think of the other characters. My favourite film for years and years was *Tom Jones*, with Albert Finney in the title role. I loved the way he'd turn to the camera and share a few thoughts with the cinema audience before the action moved on. Keith telling Clive, the cameraman, exactly what to point at made the scene so much more personal and immediate, and it turned Clive into a house-hold name. 'Over here, Clive. Come up to me, Clive. Over there, Clive ...' became a hallmark of the show. What Floyd had done, in fact, was make the audience become more involved, because he wasn't just directing the camera, he was directing the viewer's eye on to what was important. It was something new, something that you could never have orchestrated. It was just Floyd's inimitable style. And actually, it was very useful, too, since in those early days I still hadn't quite worked out how to cover the entire cooking process with just one camera. It all chimed perfectly with the foremost maxim in the world, which is: 'The simple things are the best.'

PART II

Just for starters

Food plays such a huge part of my life; it dominates my work and, at the risk of sounding tedious, quite a bit of my conversation. In fact, I don't think I've got any friends who aren't interested in food. They say that the average male thinks about sex every four minutes, well I reckon I think about food – and occasionally sex – every four minutes. I'll drift off and think about pies, the kind of rabbit pies with mustard that my mother used to make shortly after the war. In the Seventies, when television executives started to discuss the possibilities of breakfast television, I thought at first it was going to be a series about people cooking breakfasts around the world. I was quite disappointed when it turned out to be a daily news magazine.

But back then my knowledge of food was limited. I hadn't lived in a little town in Provence and, unlike Keith, I had learnt about things like salamis, olives, bread, and wine from choosing and trying stuff from the aisles and counters of the new Carrefour supermarket which had opened up in Bristol. Because I enjoyed cooking so much my friends thought me quite sophisticated, but until then I had never smelt a truffle, let alone eaten one. Caviar was a complete mystery to me and I thought sweetbreads were bull's testicles.

One of the things we shared from our childhood, though, was a love of catching fish, mainly trout, and cooking it in the fresh air: Keith, as a young boy, growing up in Somerset, fishing on a reservoir near Wiveliscombe, and me, with my friends, Bob Lipscombe and his brother Michael, fishing on parts of the River Itchen that flowed from beyond Winchester to Southampton. Subconsciously, I think this was why we filmed so many cooking sequences outside. It was never really discussed; it just happened.

I think the Itchen is the most beautiful river in the country with its gin-clear water and waving beds of weed, the perfect environment for the handsome speckled brown trout which would lie almost motionless, save for the movement of their tails keeping them in position against the swift current. On weekends and summer evenings the three of us boys would spend our time playing on the banks and fishing. We had to pluck up courage because we weren't supposed to be there. The river was strictly off limits and could only be fished by very rich people who paid to use large stretches of it in the summer. Technically we were poachers, albeit small time, but nevertheless we were breaking the law of the land. We local lads thought it our natural right to catch the odd trout from the river that flowed past our homes, even if the landowners and their water bailiffs didn't see it that way.

One of the most feared water bailiffs was called Arthur. He had a large white Alsatian dog and was thought to carry a shotgun in which the cartridges were loaded with salt crystals instead of lead shot. The word was that they stung mightily. Arthur was the keeper of the salmon pool – this was where the freshwater of the River Itchen met the salty water of the Solent and it smelt of seaweed. Sometimes, through chain-link fencing, we'd watch the people who had paid for the privilege of fishing this magical spot as if they were an exotic species in a zoo. We could see that some of them weren't particularly fussed about fishing and would prefer to sit and chat over sandwiches or a cigarette. What a waste of precious time.

Sometimes the silvery salmon would jump clear out of the water and, as if in slow motion, they would almost come to a stop before they fell back into the dark waters. We would watch like cats gazing at birds through a window, shivering with excitement. When the temptation proved too much the three of us would go out in the early morning to fish the water meadows that ran for miles along the banks of the Itchen. They were criss-crossed by small streams and sometimes little bridges made out of red brick overgrown with grass. Other times the water would be forced through a series of sluices before it rushed into a deep pool fringed with yellow and purple irises and kingcups.

In this flat landscape we could see for a mile in any direction. Any figure we spotted on the horizon made our hearts beat faster. A dog, especially a black Labrador or an Alsatian, might mean a bailiff was close by and it was time to run, though, fortunately, this stretch of water was off limits for Arthur and his fearsome white dog.

By baiting a small bronze hook with a worm and gently trotting it downstream underneath the overhanging blackthorn bushes, we could catch brown trout. They weren't very big, about half a pound, but they were strong fighters and it was a pleasure to land them.

Once we'd caught two or three we'd to go back to the den we'd made from old bits of corrugated iron and tarpaulin. It was in a wood close to where we lived, next to a muddy, scruffy tidal tributary of the Itchen, where people used to dump their old prams. We'd thread sharpened twigs through each trout from head to tail and grill them over a camp fire, turning them so the skin cooked evenly.

To eat with them we'd make a thing called a twist. We would mix up some flour and water and knead it to make a dough. Then we'd twist it round a stick – hence the name – and put it over the fire where it would bubble and blister and eventually go smoky black. We'd cut it up with our sheath knives, sprinkle the pieces with salt, add a knob of butter and wow! If my mother had served up hot black dough and undercooked fish at home I'd have seriously considered running away, but out there in our beloved camp with our eyes stinging and streaming from the smoke, they tasted wonderful. Such are the pleasures of eating outdoors.

I think my fixation with food began in the days of rationing shortly after the war. Rationing continued for nearly ten years after the war had ended; in effect, the first ten years of my life. There wasn't much food about, apart from parsnips, tripe, rissoles, rabbits for those quite wonderful pies, herrings and pilchards. I had no idea what rationing was, of course; the only thing I knew was that food was to be eaten and not necessarily enjoyed – although for the most part I did enjoy it – and that the little buff-coloured ration book was the source of my mother's culinary woes. I suppose this was the period of the line 'You're not going to get down from the table until you've eaten every last thing on your plate.'

There were exceptions to this rather dull food. Sometimes my mother would be given a couple of pounds of pork chipolatas by the local butcher. (She played in the local whist drive with his wife.) Other times we would catch the bus and visit one my mother's friends who lived in the country. This was an altogether better world where we'd be given boiled ham with parsley sauce and fresh broad beans from their amply stocked garden. The people who lived in the countryside were a lot better off than those in the towns and cities. They would feed their hens with boiled peelings from the vegetables, mixed with bran, and the malty smell was overwhelmingly delicious, just like the smell from a brewery. I couldn't resist trying the mixture. It would have been better with a little butter and a dusting of white pepper, but it was better than tripe and better than liver. Lucky hens.

These were the days of tripe and offal, sticky spoonfuls of malt, concentrated orange juice that came in medicine bottles with corks, tins of condensed milk (a luxury), and cod liver oil; but from time to time something rare and beautiful would appear in the middle of the dining table: steak and kidney pudding, in a big white bowl covered with a tea towel, tied with string. It was a memory I'd play over and over just before going to sleep: the sight of a large spoon disappearing into that pale golden suet pastry and then coming up with a steaming mound of steak and kidney in rich velvety gravy. It was the stuff of my dreams.

My earliest memory of food was when I was learning to read. It was an illustrated fairy tale about a village that grew a giant turnip. It grew and grew until it overshadowed the cottages. In the end the blacksmith made a huge cauldron and the whole village feasted on a delicious turnip soup for days to come. The illustrations looked so lovely, with bits of the purple and yellow turnip, with its green leaves, simmering away while the villagers sprinkled it with pepper and gazed longingly at it and drooled. Even reading books like *Treasure Island* stimulated my appetite when, in the opening chapter, Billy Bones, a drunken pirate captain, stops at an inn and asks for a plate of bacon and eggs. Apparently that's all he wanted to eat, a plate of bacon and eggs, and a bottle of rum. Forget the rum, I used to spend some time conjuring up what a plate of bacon and eggs would look like. I don't think four ounces of rashers, the permissible weekly amount then, would have covered the plate.

Even singing Christmas carols in the church choir made me feel hungry. 'Bring me flesh and bring me wine,' said the carol 'Good King Wenceslas', and I'd imagine hunks of meat roasting on a spit in a huge fireplace with flagons of red wine nearby – an image no doubt equally inspired by a film I'd never tire of seeing at the Savoy cinema in Swaythling on Saturday afternoons: *Robin Hood*. I loved the way the Merry Men would eat using a dagger, ripping the meat with their hands with lots of enthusiastic grunting. Then they'd quaff goblets of wine and, because their mouths were so full, it ran down their chins, the director's way of painting a picture of a Saxon peasant living in a land of plenty. By contrast the ever grumpy Sheriff of Nottingham would just pick at his food and have the occasional grape. I used to come out of that cinema in the late afternoon feeling ravenous and wishing I could have exactly what Robin, Little John, and Friar Tuck had, including vast goblets of wine, but in all probability I'd be sitting down to a pilchard salad and a Cremola Foam.

Is there anything better than jam roly-poly?

The food at school may not have been popular with most of the children, but for me it was still the highlight of every day. All puddings were welcome, but jam roly-poly was more welcome than anything else. At the age of ten I was sent away to Wedges School in Sussex. It was for sickly children from poor families and although it was in a neighbouring county it was run by the health department of Hampshire County Council. Along with lots of children I suffered from asthma; in the hot summer months the panicky bouts of breathlessness became worse and more frequent. The only relief I, and thousands of other kids, had back then was to breathe into a pretty scary black plastic face mask which had a small rubber hand pump attached to the bottom of it. After ten minutes or so, breathing became easier and I would drift gently into a deep impenetrable sleep.

Wedges was a collection of large, wooden-framed dormitory huts and ablution blocks set around playing fields with an admin building, theatre, and a large canteen positioned near the entrance. It was a slightly more cheerful version of a Stalag Luft camp, without the watchtowers and barbed wire, and I suspect it must have been built by the military during, or shortly after, the war. When not in the classroom the pupils would be in the surrounding fields doing star jumps, deep breathing exercises and gentle cross-country runs, because this was a 'fresh air school', part of an incentive by the government to help children breath fresh, clean country air.

Meat rationing had finally come to an end and precooked meat, sliced and reheated in thin, greasy gravy, was served nearly every day. Boys of ten years didn't know the difference between beef and lamb or, for that matter, pork and chicken, when it was cooked and presented in such a way. It was always accompanied by mashed potatoes that had the consistency of wallpaper paste. There must have been a mountain the size of Everest made up of powdered mashed potatoes untouched from the last war. One of the best commercials ever made was the one for instant mashed potato in the Seventies – lots of metal Martians laughing so much at the report of some poor bloke who was peeling a potato, cooking it for twenty minutes, then smashing it to bits, that they fell off their chairs. All I can say is that the product celebrated by the merry Martians was as bad as it was in my schooldays.

Stuffed heart and 'beef olives' weren't very popular with most of the children, but I loved them. They were packed with the familiar and reassuring taste of home – Paxo stuffing. I know it's frowned on by the gourmets of today, but I would put Paxo, along with HP sauce, Branston pickle and Colman's mustard powder, on my culinary version of *Desert Island Discs*, if there were one. Steak and kidney pie and Spam fritters were the stuff of dreams and any meat dish with dumplings in it was worth breaking into a trot for, to get to the counter first.

In the days before Captain Birdseye most fish was unloved by children, so baked herrings were seriously unpopular, as were fish stews, but there were three exceptions: fish pie, fish cakes, and fish and chips. Boiled cabbage was universally disliked, but I happened to love it and regularly used to eat everyone else's leftovers: lovely with gravy, white pepper, and a dash of malt vinegar. In those days all pepper was white, all salt came from the Saxo factory miles away from the sea and all the vinegar was malt. 'Don't say vinegar – say Sarson's.'

But nothing in that strange, makeshift school in 1955 gave so much pleasure as puddings, which were eaten at breakneck speed in case the master in charge of the dining room gave the call for second helpings. One of our favourites was chocolate sponge with lashings of hot chocolate custard – a new invention – but by far the tastiest, sweetest and the fairest of them all was jam roly-poly. When I watch wildlife films on television I can totally identify with the wild beast who rushes away with a leg of antelope, his eyes darting everywhere until he finds a hidden lair where he can tuck in without fear of it being snatched away, because I felt like that about jam roly-poly. I would eat mine slowly, savouring every sticky jammy mouthful, whilst others rushed theirs in the hope of getting seconds. Of course, I knew there wouldn't be an invitation for second helpings, because like chocolate sponge, treacle pudding, and apple pie, jam roly-poly was just too good. Tapioca – the stuff that looks like frogspawn – now that's a different story altogether.

I ran away from school once with Clive, my best friend. I wasn't really unhappy at Wedges but I did miss my mother and Clive missed his monkey. His father was a seaman who brought an African grass monkey back from one of his trips. That's what merchant seamen did in those days: they brought home parakeets and parrots, chameleons and mynah birds. Meanwhile the stevedores returned home from the docks with bananas, oranges and lots of exotic fruit, which came from the crates that 'accidentally' crashed onto the quayside from the cranes unloading the cargo ships. It was considered a perk of the job in the days before container ships were invented – maybe that's *why* they were invented. In the school play-ground, you could always spot the son of a docker because he was the one with the pomegranates.

It was a taste for a small adventure, coupled with a visit from my mother, which probably triggered the need to get back home. She looked very tired and sad when she visited me one weekend. Wedges School wasn't an easy place to get to and she had to catch several trains and buses. For a special treat she took me to lunch at a place called The Carfax in Horsham, where we had fish and chips. This was my very first visit to a restaurant – I'd seen lots of them in films – and it made me feel very grown-up indeed. There were waitresses in frilly hats and black dresses with white aprons, and there was tea in silver pots. Intrigued by its strange name I had mock turtle soup, a beef consommé with bits of meat floating about in it, to start; followed by plaice, fried in bread-crumbs, with chips, peas, and a wedge of lemon in a silver squeezer (I'd never set eyes on one of those before), and bread and butter. It was here my mother told me that she and my father were no longer married because he had gone away with another lady and wouldn't be coming home any more. Actually, she didn't use the word lady.

I could hardly remember seeing my father. He worked for the Customs and Excise in Weymouth and rarely came home to Southampton, so this news wasn't partic-ularly hurtful to me, except it made me feel deeply sorry for my mother having to travel all that way back home on her own. I heard years later, through a chance meeting with a retired Customs officer in a pub, that what had happened was that my father had given a couple of attrac-tive women a ride around Weymouth Bay on his Customs launch. They had mistaken him for the harbour master and asked him if he knew where they might find a boat. He told them he had the perfect vessel for such a trip and a few years later he ended up marrying one of the women, who was extremely sophisticated and beautiful and bought silks for Liberty's, the famous shop in London; so different from my mother, who rode a moped.

The plan for running away from school was to head for the nearest railway station and then home, or rather to

Portsmouth first where Clive's family lived, because I really wanted to see his monkey. We left shortly after breakfast, just before classes began, and we took with us some sliced bread and Dairylea cheese triangles, Penguin biscuits, and fruit. It seemed more than enough. We had no map and no sense of direction, but it felt really good to run through the woods of silver birch and oak trees that separated the villages of Barns Green and Five Oaks. We were looking for signs to Horsham, because I was sure it was bound to have a railway station – not that we had any money to buy tickets, but we were ten years old, full of optimism and would cross that bridge when we came to it. Actually some things never change, because I still think like that.

In the woods we found an old ruined bungalow. It was overgrown with silver birch, ivy, and other plants and the roof had long since gone. It even had a swimming pool that still had traces of sky blue paint, but it was full of rubbish and dead leaves. Naturally, as ten-year-olds, we thought we'd find some treasure in a posh place with a pool. We spent ages picking our way from one room to another but apart from some buckled saucepans and a rotting armchair everything of value had been taken long ago. Maybe it was hit by a bomb during the war or it was the scene of an unsolved murder where everyone was killed: the murder in the woods.

After that we found an old disused barn made of brick and above one of the windows was a crest with a red cow on it. I thought that it would be so nice to take it back home to give to my mother, so that she could put it on her mantelpiece. It took ages to prise it off the wall and because it was cast iron it was very heavy. We took turns carrying it but tiredness had altered our mood and eventually we dumped it in a bush. After several hours on the run, we were most definitely lost. As the afternoon wore on we could start to smell the wood smoke from the cottages which signalled the end of the day. The bread and the cheese triangles, the fruit and the precious Penguins hadn't lasted very long after all and by this time we were extremely tired, ravenously hungry and a trifle tearful.

We were now free of the woods and were walking along the main road near Billingshurst when miraculously we were picked up by Mr Woods, the deputy headmaster, in his Austin Big Seven saloon. All thoughts of getting home had long gone. The only adventure we wanted now was with a large plate of stew or Spam fritters, chips, and beans. Now that would be something.

On arrival at the school we were taken to Mr Booth, the headmaster, expecting, at best, a bit of an ear-wigging, at worst, serious punishment; maybe the cane. His office was at the front of the main hall and it had a wooden balcony which overlooked the large playground. The main hall doubled as a theatre and cinema. A couple of weeks before we'd run away, I'd sung 'If you Knew Susie Like I Know Susie' to the whole school as part of a show put on by our dormitory. I was really nervous and I'd managed to get through the first verse without overexciting the audience when suddenly I'd had a brilliant thought. I'd continue the rest of the song imitating the voice of Bluebottle from the *Goon Show*. We spent most of our time at school talking like Bluebottle, Neddie

Seagoon, Major Bloodnok, Eccles and Minnie Bannister until our throats were hoarse. It proved the right decision and I had wanted to stay on the stage all evening. Eventually I was hauled off.

Surprisingly, when we were handed over to the headmaster for punishment we were treated with great sympathy and understanding. Apparently Mr Booth had learnt that my parents had recently divorced, which he thought extremely tragic. Divorce was a much rarer phenomenon in 1955 than today and considered far more catastrophic and devastating for the children involved. The dormitory mistress, Miss Luquot, was there with tears in her eyes, listening to this kind and wise man giving counsel. He could fully understand why an only child would wish to return home as quickly as possible in these troubled times to be by his mother's side. He thought my friend Clive very loyal, if not a little foolhardy, for keeping me company on my journey home. Both of us gazed downwards, studying the knot holes in the floor, looking suitably sorry for ourselves, hoping that the ordeal would soon be over and there would be some food left in the refectory – maybe even jam roly-poly. Through some form of telepathy we both thought it best, under the circumstances, not to mention the monkey.

The best of British

I had stayed at Wedges School for three terms and came back to Southampton in time to fail my eleven plus. It wasn't surprising really, because the emphasis for the past year had been on health and nature studies. I knew all about moths and butterflies, wild flowers and trees. I knew how to make rosehip syrup, put up a tent and make a campfire, but my knowledge of decimals and algebra and conjugated verbs was somewhat limited. So, back in Southampton I started at Mayfield Road Secondary Modern. It was a world apart from the woods and fields that engulfed Wedges and there was a great difference in attitude among the children. Bullying was rife and the building was so old there were no facilities for school dinners. So lunchtimes meant a quick bicycle ride to the grocer's for a cold Miller's steak and kidney pie, a delicious bargain at just ten pence each: that's less than 5p in today's money. Sometimes lunch would consist of five Player's Weights cigarettes and a shared bottle of New Forest Brown Ale. But best of all was fish and chips. Is there anything better than piping hot fish and chips and the smell of vinegar on hot beef dripping as you walk along the road with your mates?

My mother was working as a receptionist in one of the halls of residence at Southampton University and I was constantly reminded by her that times were very hard indeed. If we were lucky enough to have a roast while listening to the *Billy Cotton Band Show* on a Sunday, it was usually a small shoulder of lamb or belly pork with apple sauce. Our neighbours, the Hunt family, who lived over the other side of the fence at the bottom of the garden, quite often had roast chicken, which was regarded as a luxury, and this used to irritate my mother.

'They want for nothing those people,' she'd say, after I told her the Hunts were having chicken again. I'd seen it come out of the oven when I had been there playing with their son, Peter. 'That's the third time they've had chicken since Christmas, and it's not even March.'

The Hunts also had a car, a telephone, parquet flooring which smelt of lavender polish, instead of lino, a serving hatch, a refrigerator, a radiogram, and, joy of joys, a twenty-one-inch television set that seemed like Cinemascope. Peter, who was my age, even had a Dansette Junior record player in his bedroom, where he played the Andrews Sisters over and over again. He went to King Edward's Grammar School and his older brother Barry flew Vulcan bombers that carried H bombs. These were the days when the Cold War was at its chilliest.

It was also the time of 'the front room', which was always cold and cheerless and, as if by some common consent, would contain a matching three-piece suite and, often, in a proletarian statement of wealth and one-upmanship, an embroidered firescreen and a cabinet displaying the best china. We didn't have the cabinet, the firescreen, or the refrigerator. We had a meat safe – a perforated metal cupboard which allowed the air to circulate. Every week the ice man would come in his green lorry which dripped water from the melting ice at an alarming rate. My mother would buy a large chunk for a few pence and the ice man, with his huge castiron tongs, would put a block into the meat safe, but after two or three days it had all melted.

It was at the Hunts' that I experienced my first taste of luxury. It was bread and butter, but not as I'd had it before. The butter was almost white and tasted like sweet cream. It was called Lurpak and I loved it. I thought of asking my mother to buy some, instead of the usual Anchor butter, but I stopped myself because I knew what the answer would be.

'They've got everything in the world those people. They've got money to burn and you expect me, on the little I earn, working my fingers to the bone, to buy some fancy butter? Think yourself lucky, young man, that you've got butter on the table at all. Most children your age don't know what butter is. Their parents give them margarine. So I don't want to hear what the high and mighty blinkin' Hunts have got, otherwise you can go and live with them!'

Actually, I thought, I'd quite like that for a while, because Peter had a lovely sister called Barbara and I worshipped her.

My mother didn't use recipe books. If she wanted to try something new she would cut recipes out of the *Southern Evening Echo* or *Woman's Realm*. I suppose cooking in the late Fifties was regarded very much as a chore, something that simply had to be done, and it was always the woman's responsibility. So my mother was as likely to buy a book about all the various ways you could cook the evening meal as one on the best means to mow the grass or clean the chimney. But I think any dietician today would say that the meals my mother cooked for very little money, week in and week out, were pretty well balanced and nutritious, especially by today's often pathetic standards.

Mondays meant curried leftovers from the Sunday lunch, made with Sharwood's curry powder from a khaki-coloured tin whose lid had to be prised off with a penny, sliced apples, onions, and the obligatory sultanas and desiccated coconut. Years later when I'd left school and started work I went to my first Indian restaurant opposite the Gaumont theatre in Southampton. What was presented to me wasn't curry as I knew it. The chicken still had its bones in and the reddish brown sauce was thick, oily and not a pale khaki. The rice had bits of pink and yellow in it – what on earth was that? There wasn't even a hint of apple and a distinct absence of sultanas and desiccated coconut. And it was hot, so hot that the pain on my tongue seemed to increase with every gulp of cold lager. I remember getting quite panicky but the friend I was with told me this was quite normal. Days after, surprisingly, I found myself longing for another curry – maybe just a fraction hotter.

Today, some fifty years later, my mother still uses Mr Sharwood's curry powder, apples, sultanas and desiccated coconut, even though I've told her a hundred times that's not the way I've seen it made in Bangladesh or Goa, Sri Lanka or Thailand. But, in her book, if it hasn't got apples and sultanas in it, it isn't curry.

Tuesday usually meant liver and as soon as I smelt it cooking my heart would sink. This was a dish that turned my stomach. Because money was so tight, my mother bought the cheapest ox liver. It was full of veins and arteries as thick and tough as the brake cables on my bike and it tasted bitter. It would be decades before I discovered that liver could be sweet and tender if it came from a lamb or a pig.

Wednesday might be a mid-week snack like Welsh rabbit or rarebit, very often served with a couple of poached eggs (apparently that's called a buck rabbit). I especially loved the way it huffed and puffed when it came from under the grill with brown and black blisters of cheese giving off a waft of beer and mustard.

Normally, about once a week, that old standby, tripe and onions poached gently in milk, would rear its head. It was never a popular visitor to my mother's kitchen because it gave off a terrible smell as it simmered on the stove. It also had a curious texture, like fish but more slippery; but served with buttery mashed potatoes and bombarded with white pepper and lashings of malt vinegar it was rather good. We might be in the middle of a resurgence of British traditional food but it would surprise me greatly if tripe ever became popular again. I can see the obituary in the *Daily Telegraph* in a year or so proclaiming 'Last tripe eater in the country dies, aged 103.'

Thursday – the day *The Beano* came out and therefore a happy day – we might have braised steak and onions with mashed potato and spring greens. I loved this much derided cornerstone of British cuisine: meat and two veg, one of them always being potatoes. My mother used one of the cheapest cuts of beef, seasoned and simmered slowly in the oven with onions that would practically disappear into the gravy, and the sweet and silky spring green is still my favourite vegetable, despite being so underrated, especially in restaurants.

Fridays, in the winter months, meant herring fillets dusted in seasoned flour and fried in butter. They'd be served with malt vinegar and accompanied by slices of Mother's Pride, lashings of Anchor butter, and a cup of tea. Always the cheapest fish on the fishmonger's slab, the herrings were creamy and satisfying. In the summer we would have a tinned pilchard salad. There's something magical and old-fashioned about a home-grown salad. Food snobs see the traditional British salad of the late Fifties as the culinary equivalent of an Ealing comedy, preferring raw fennel, chicory, and rocket to its trusty cast of soft round lettuce, cucumber, spring onions, radishes, tomatoes, beetroot, and boiled eggs – and, of course, Heinz salad cream. However, our neighbours the Hunts, who spent their holidays abroad, would probably have preferred mayonnaise.

On Saturday we might have something luxurious and very grown-up, like a grilled cod cutlet with slices of tomato on top; but Sunday was the day that smelt differently to any other day. On Sunday the whole country was engulfed in the aroma of roast dinner – nobody then called it lunch. If any foreign power had wanted to attack Britain then one o'clock on a Sunday would have been the perfect time, because everyone was preoccupied with sitting down to the traditional roast. Even the sounds were different on a Sunday. Accompanying the church bells would be the metallic scrape of carving knives being sharpened on concrete back doorsteps. In the summer when the windows were open, you'd hear *Family Favourites* played from every radio in the street, punctuated with letters from soldiers serving in Cyprus, Germany, Kenya, and Hong Kong.

Vegetarians hadn't yet been invented, at least not in our neighbourhood. But accompanying the roast pork and apple sauce would be a staggering amount of vegetables: mashed swede, roast potatoes and parsnips, spring cabbage, carrots, marrow, and probably peas. And over this delicious mountain range would be poured the gravy made from the meat juices mixed with water from the vegetables and thickened with flour and a spoonful or two of Bisto. The Yorkshire puddings would fill like lakes, and ravines would form down the hills of mashed swede. As far as I'm concerned this is the Holy Grail of food. Nothing can beat a Sunday dinner – I mean lunch.

PART III

Panzer division

My first job in television was working in a film vault in Southampton, a silver tunnel made up of film cans which made me feel at times that I was slowly going mad inside in a metal tube. The vault contained all the commercials that were shown on Southern Television in 1963, the year in which Philip Larkin said sexual intercourse was invented.

Getting into television at all was a matter of luck. Having left school with just O level art, I went to Southampton Technical College to resit all six of my other exams. This time I failed them all again, except history. Simultaneously I studied part-time at Southampton College of Art. I saw myself as a famous designer of book covers. These were the days when paperback thrillers were in their heyday and the covers I liked best were a cross between film noir and pulp (have you noticed the cover of this book?). After a while, though, it became apparent that the other students' rough sketches were so much better than my finished work, and I realized I was utterly useless at the subject. So I left and got a temporary job on a building site while I figured out what to do next. I was climbing a ladder one day when my mother came by on her moped, waving at me. Apparently she'd seen a wonderful job advertised in the *Evening Echo*: Assistant In Film at Southern Television.

'You must apply for it David. You've always said you want to work in television,' she said.

So I wrote off to Southern Television, the local ITV company that served the south of England, saying I wanted desperately to be an Assistant In Film. Whatever that was. And I got an interview. They were interviewing eighty people for just one job, and they offered it to *me*. Only the job turned out not to be an Assistant In Film but a vault porter. When I asked why they hadn't advertised the job as vault porter, they said, 'Well, nobody would apply would they?'

As was the case with all independent companies that made up ITV at the time, advertisements were the bread and butter of Southern Television, and I was paid five pounds a week to look after them. There were thousands of the bloody things forming the lining to my silver tunnel, or tomb, as I used to call it, and each had a number and had to be returned to its rightful place once it had been shown. I'd spend most of my day dusting them and making sure they were in the right order.

In the early Sixties, TV commercials were as popular as the hit programmes like *Emergency Ward 10*, *Dr. Kildare*, *The Avengers*, *Dr Who*, *Coronation Street*, and, best of all, *Danger Man*. Many of the ads were exotic and sophisti-cated, like the one for Fry's Turkish Delight featuring scantily clad girls 'full of Eastern promise'. Then there were the James Bond-style spoofs advertising Schweppes, in which a suave William Franklin would whisper 'Schhh … you know who.' However, the majority of them were about overworked mums so happy with their cleaning fluid they'd end up dancing round their vast spotless kitchens with mops. There were other glamorous young mums who became dreamy eyed because 'Hands that do dishes can feel soft as your face with mild green Fairy Liquid'. Some of the ads starred iconic characters like the Dulux dog, or had ongoing stories featuring families, like Katie and Philip in the series of Oxo advertisements. My favourite was the one in which Philip phoned his pretty wife Katie and said that he was bringing his boss home for dinner – and his wife was coming too. Katie, who always looked so nice in her starched blouses and neat hair (a bit like Delia), said, with a cheeky grin, 'That's all right darling. I'll think of something.' And she made a lovely beef bourguignon, but, of course, it was the beef gravy that made it so memorable, because we saw her crumbling the cube with her delicate fingers and giving the camera a little wink. In fact, it was so good Philip got promoted the very next day, a piece of news that really didn't come as much of a surprise to Katie. It was all thanks to Oxo.

There were nearly three thousand of these little films housed in this airless void; some just cheerful nonsense, some of them quite brilliant, like the PG Tips tea commercials, starring the Tipps family of chimps dressed as humans, which made it into the *Guinness Book of Records* for the UK's longest-running TV ad. Some had catchphrases and jingles that stayed in your head like 'You'll wonder where the yellow went when you brush your teeth with Pepsodent', at the end of an ad featuring the cartoon characters Suzy Q and the gang; Murray Mints, the 'too good to hurry mints'; Opal Fruits, 'made to make our mouth water'; 'Keep going well, keep going Shell' sung by none other than Bing Crosby, or 'Bom, Bom, Bom, Bom, Esso Blue!' I found out later that most of these were written by two men, Johnny Johnston, the King of the Jingles, and Cliff Adams.

I was eighteen and I'd only been at Southern Television for a few months when I was invited to the annual Christmas party held in the ballroom at the Royal Pier in Southampton. It was an extremely glamorous occasion at which most of the men were dressed in dinner suits and the women had transformed themselves into film stars. I sat at the film department table in my new C&A blazer and grey flannels and gave up trying to eat my soup because my hand was shaking so much with nerves. This was the grandest thing I'd ever set eyes on and I was part of it.

I was halfway through buttering my bread roll when one of the film editors, a freelance called Tony Childs, said to me in his public school accent: 'Look, it's pretty clear you haven't been to one of these things before, because it looks to me like you're making sandwiches for the school cricket team.'

Well, it was true that I had split the roll down the middle and had started buttering it before this impromptu lesson in etiquette.

'What you do,' he said, 'is break off the bread like so,' tearing off a piece the size of a walnut. 'Butter it like so and pop it into the old gob.'

By the time he'd finished I'd turned bright red and thought my head would explode with embarrassment. Previously, I'd thought that there were only two rules on eating: don't talk with your mouth full and keep your elbows off the table.

I discovered a number of things that night. First, the meat of a roast turkey, something I'd never tasted before, was suspiciously dark and had a strong, foreign smell, quite unlike chicken. Second, and I was told this by the man who showed me how to eat a bread roll, those were not Smith's potato crisps accompanying the other vegetables on the plate – they were called 'game chips'. Third, wine was so sour it was undrinkable, though I quickly realized it was supposed to taste like that, and actually it was exceedingly good. And finally, C&A blazers, even with silver buttons, don't really cut the mustard at such a function. Bernadette from the accounts department, whom I worshipped, didn't once look in my direction. Instead, she spent the entire evening laughing and dancing with some cameraman with a suntan, who was much older than her; he must have been at least twenty-five. Such was the power of the dinner jacket and bow tie, I thought. The experience reminded me of when I made the occasional appearance in my secondary modern school cricket team. Our outfits would consist of white shirts, Royal Navy surplus shorts and white plimsolls. Sometimes we would play the local grammar school and the game would be over before it had even begun once we saw our well-spoken opponents dressed immaculately in cricket whites. We didn't stand a chance.

My job as vault porter didn't exactly make me feel a part of this world of presenters, producers, cameramen, set designers, make-up ladies, floor managers, and reporters, some of them household names. Instead it made me sound as if I would have fitted better into Bram Stoker's *Dracula*.

My world was buried deep in the heart of an old converted cinema in Southampton, more or less in the front stalls. Every day I was given a list of commercials on 35mm film to take out of the vault and give to the five ladies who would sit all day long at their work benches, splicing each advert together onto huge reels. Once the reels were complete I'd carry them down to the telecine machines, which would transmit them in the commercial breaks throughout the evening's programmes. Then it was back to the dusting and cataloguing. At the end of each day I felt rather like a hermit with long straggly hair and saucer eyes who stumbles from a vast cave in some biblical Hollywood epic. But there were two brilliant things about this job. The first was the canteen which made the most wonderful steak and kidney pies and macaroni cheese, and the second was that the vault was in the department where the film editors worked.

To me the film editors were gods who were paid lots of money for doing something really creative. They had sports cars and glamorous girlfriends and they bought their clothes in Carnaby Street in London. They wore Chelsea boots, suede jackets, polo neck sweaters and button-down shirts. They modelled themselves on Georgie Fame and Paul McCartney and they smelt expensive. Not at all like my friends in Swaythling who ponged of Old Spice, the most popular aftershave, and everyone's favourite Christmas present in those days.

As soon as I finished my work in the dreaded vault, I'd ask the film editors for their permission to watch them at work. The most charismatic of all the editors at Southern Television in the mid-Sixties was a colossus of a man called Mike Connor. He was the nephew of the highly respected *Daily Mirror* columnist, William Connor, more famously known as Cassandra. Such was his immense personality and *joie de vivre* it was said that no party, of which there were many, could possibly start without him. Not only was he an editor, but he made his own films for the nightly magazine show, *Day by Day*. From time to time he'd allow me to sit at the back of the cutting room providing I didn't say anything – 'one word and you're out' was the deal.

On one occasion he'd been filming on a pirate radio station for a weekend, finding out what life was like for the disc jockeys on-board a converted ferry anchored off the south-east coast. At that time the government was pretty fed up with these naughty pirate radio stations. They grumbled that these ships posed a danger for seafarers and they wanted them closed down. You don't have to be terribly cynical to suspect the real reason for their continued annoyance might well have been that they were missing out on a fortune's worth of taxable advertising revenue. Millions upon millions of young people were listening to Radios Caroline and London, ignoring the daily offerings from the BBC's Light Programme.

If anything epitomized the rebellious spirit of the Sixties – apart from the Rolling Stones and Harold Wilson's raincoat – then it was Radio Caroline, with its sexy signature tune and unscripted performances by its DJs. There was a general feeling it wouldn't be around much longer, so Mike Connor persuaded the powers at Southern Television to let him make his film before it disappeared. He chose a good time to go because the weather looked horrendous, with plates and bottles sliding off tables and high waves crashing over the side.

I would sit and watch him knit pieces of interview together with music and footage of life on-board. He chose the Beatles' 'We Can Work It Out' to use as a musical thread throughout the little film. It was curious and, I suspect, quite lucky, the way that the lyrics fitted the pictures so well, especially over scenes where the disc jockeys – Tony Blackburn and Johnnie Walker (I think) – were trying to eat a meal in a force-eight gale and laughing their heads off. This surely was the rite of passage for any disc jockey worth his salt in the mid-Sixties, a world away from the nice chaps in suits and Pringle sweaters who represented the BBC's idea of youth culture at the time.

Radio Caroline was powerful stuff for me and I loved the way this film bounced along using music and people telling their own stories of life on-board without any presenters and reporters. If I could have pressed a magic button there and then and sold my soul to the devil to become a film editor, without hesitation, I would have done so. This was what I wanted to do.

Once Mike had finished cutting the film, which he did so speedily, it then had to be seen by the journalist in charge of the programme, an extremely hard-working man called Ken Seymour. Ken would start work before anyone else and he'd read all the papers, both national and local, before the rest of the staff turned up. There were still a couple of hours to go before transmission, and there was a degree of tension in the air. Unfortunately, Mr Seymour thought Mike's film far too long and told him to cut it down by five minutes. The film only ran for ten, so he'd have to ditch so much good material, which would inevitably ruin his impression of life on-board this iconic ship.

Then something happened that took me completely by surprise. Mike's hand shot out, grabbed Mr Seymour by the knot of his tie, and then he stood up, taking the unfortunate journalist with him. It was as if he was escorting a naughty puppy from the room after he'd made a mess on the new carpet. Poor Ken was marched the length of the film department and unceremoniously flung out, followed by his clipboard.

'Fucking journos,' said Connor.

I was speechless. Was it like this all the time?

A few minutes later, as if in a scene from a Gilbert and Sullivan operetta, the management, led by the editor, Terry Johnston, came marching up the stairs to the film department. These were the suited, pinstriped, braces-wearing bosses, and to me they looked pretty scary. I think at that moment I would have preferred to be in my silver vault dusting the film cans, and not exposed in this den of revolution. Like Panzers crossing the Polish border they marched straight to Mike's cutting room and slammed the door so hard I thought the frosted glass might have fallen out. Unbeknown to me at the time, what I was witnessing was the clash as one culture began to get to grips with another. ITV wasn't even ten years old when this incident happened, and for many of the older film editors, who had come to work in television from a documentary, feature film, and cinema background, and regarded themselves as artists, the 'news magazine' was something that took a bit of getting used to. They despised the world of journalism.

Terry Johnston was a formidable man with a glass eye who was thought of by his peers as one of the best TV magazine editors in the country. Some of the film editors, and me, tried to eavesdrop on what was being said behind the opaque glass, but the film had started to play on the editing machine. Much to our amazement Mr Johnston and his friends seemed to like the film and didn't insist on any changes. What a result. As soon as the door handle started to turn, we scurried off like naughty rabbits. Mr Johnston pulled his master stroke when he was just about to leave.

In full view of virtually everyone in the department he glared at Mike with his one working eye and said: 'If you ever lay a hand on one of my journalists again I'll have you out of here so fast, you'll never work in television again.'

There was not a scintilla of doubt that he meant every word, as the Panzers roared off back across the border from whence they came. I found out later that's called a 'quid pro quo'.

Spag bol and all that

It was around 1965 that I discovered spaghetti bolognese. The film editors regularly used to go to Margarita's, an Italian restaurant near the railway station in Southampton. I'd often hear them talk about this place. They'd come into work sporting dark glasses and feigning monstrous hangovers. I'd love to have a hangover and wear sunglasses indoors, I thought: it's so cool. They would talk with great passion about Margarita's, the size of the portions and how wonderful the owners were, and how many empty bottles were stacked up on the tables when they left. Apart from the canteen at Southern Television I'd never been to a proper restaurant, except The Carfax in Horsham, where my mother had taken me the day she told me that she and dad had divorced. As soon as we walked in I knew everything I'd heard about the place was true. Red checked tablecloths, wine bottles with candles, and Mario Lanza on the record player. There was a flurry of tables being pushed together and welcome handshakes. It was just like a scene out of one of those old black and white Hollywood gangster films starring Edward G. Robinson – except this was downtown Southampton and not Little Italy.

Even I, as a newcomer, was introduced to Margarita and the waiters. They even said, 'David, please sit down and enjoy yourself.'

It made me feel I belonged – not just in the restaurant – but in this group of people I really admired and aspired to be like. I was a little more confident in this sort of situation now, having been to a couple of wedding buffets – chunks of cheese and pineapple on cocktail sticks, vol au vents filled with a cold and suspicious mixture of creamy chicken and mushroom, sausage rolls, silver 'cocktail' onions, and sandwiches made from tinned pink salmon – but nothing prepared me for this. The plates were massive and there was a mountain of what looked like steaming white string topped with a foul smelling powder, which I later learnt was the famous Parmesan cheese, and a small forest of parsley. This was a pretty bad start; and the wine, which came in bottles wrapped in raffia, tasted like the dregs left over from long forgotten bottles of scrumpy.

It was the Walt Disney film *The Lady and the Tramp* that made me want to try spaghetti; the famous scene in which the pretty cocker spaniel and the grey mongrel are sitting under the stars next to the dustbins behind an Italian restaurant. The kindly restaurateur, realizing they're passionately in love, presents them, in true Neapolitan style, with a steaming plate of spaghetti and meatballs to share. Of course, not being able to use a fork and a spoon, the inevitable happens when they inadvertently suck at the same long strand of pasta and end up kissing. I think that moment did more for Italian food the world over than anything before or since. Remember this was 1965, and half the nation thought that spaghetti came in tins with tomato sauce and should only be eaten on toast.

Oh dear, I thought, what to do? I looked at this huge mound of pasta (the equivalent of about five large tins' worth) and then watched, searching for handy tips, as Mike, Pete, Rod, Slim, and Eddie started to eat their spaghetti. The smell of the cheese, well, it bore a strong resemblance to vomit. How could anyone make cheese that smelt like that? And where were the meatballs? And why was the spaghetti so white and quite tough? The editors started to coil the strands expertly around their forks. I copied them, hoping the strings of spaghetti would gradually come to an end, but instead ended up with a ball on my fork which looked very much like my mother's knitting. But I discovered that under the Parmesan was a meaty sauce, sadly no meatballs, but nevertheless I instantly liked it very much indeed. This was my first introduction to garlic, olive oil, herbs, and tomato sauce, not to mention the Parmesan, which after the initial shock, tasted really good – so much so that I wanted more.

The pasta, unlike the tinned stuff, had a real bite to it. There was almost an audible click when you bit through it, and it tasted buttery and satisfying even on its own. Even the wine started to taste good, and it went so well with the sauce and the pasta; it was, as I was to learn years later, all about point and counterpoint. Looking back I think this was the culinary equivalent to listening to Bill Haley and the Comets for the first time – you may not have liked everything about it, but inside you knew it was important and there was no going back to skiffle. With any luck, I could have a hangover and wear dark glasses like the rest of them in the morning.

For many people in the Sixties, spaghetti bolognese was the bridge that led to a different world of taste and flavours. Over the coming months and years there would be risotto, paella, lasagne, beef bourguignon, and coq au vin. Wine with attractive labels from Peter Dominic's would appear on the table, especially at weekends. Cheeses other than Cheddar and Danish Blue would make an appearance, such as Port Salut, Gorgonzola, and Emmental. Avocados, aubergines, and capsicums would be given a try out by the high street greengrocer. Soon there would be other types of vinegar on the shelves of the corner shop, apart from Sarson's Malt; and olive oil, previously sold at chemists in little bottles and used to loosen ear wax, would be available in certain upmarket grocers for salad dressings and cooking.

Men, who previously would never have been seen shopping for food, or shopping for anything come to that, would begin to have spirited discussions about risotto and prawn curries made with coconut milk with their friends down the pub; an idea that before the Sixties was beyond anyone's imagination. Today we're surrounded by a heady sense of gastronomic adventure which some people, admittedly, are beginning to find quite tiresome, but for many of us, it all started with spaghetti bolognese.

Thirty years later I made a pilgrimage to Bologna as part of a series I was making with Antonio Carluccio. We were on a journey throughout northern Italy and he warned me that the people in Bologna do not eat spaghetti bolognese. This was like hearing that the good burghers of Munich never drink beer and the citizens of Toulouse are not partial to the odd spicy sausage. So we went, and Antonio was right. I tried all the restaurants, cafés, and delicatessens and the reply was always the same – never spaghetti with a bolognese sauce, always tagliatelle, and always fresh, never dried.

PART IV

Proof of the pudding

I find the whole process of making films very much like cooking, which is another reason why I like it so much. As every good cook knows, creating a good meal always starts with shopping; gathering up everything you'll possibly need to make a dish. But you don't always know exactly what you are going to buy, until you see what is good.

I might have it in mind to make a fish pie, so I visit the fish stall in the market and maybe I'll pick up some cod, prawns, and some fillets of monkfish. Then, I spot the mussels, which look good, and just past the herrings, taking pride of place on the slab, are half a dozen beautifully fresh squid, landed in the middle of the night to arrive in all their pink translucent glory right in front of me. Squid and fish pie are not really made for each other, so what started out as a humble fish pie has turned, in a matter of seconds, into a paella.

Such is cooking, such is filming. You can spend weeks researching a subject and suddenly you see or hear something when you're out with the camera and you know in your heart you must have it in the programme. One of the most consistent of the many criticisms aimed at the early

Floyd programmes was that it looked as if we made it up as we went along – and, of course, we had.

Once you have your ingredients, you start putting your dish together. This is my favourite bit. Editing rooms are like kitchens where you can experiment by sticking this scene next to that, very much as an instinctive chef puts the most unlikely ingredients together to create something new. At some stage in this process it's time to season the whole dish with music. I chose the Stranglers' 'Waltz in Black' as the opening theme for Floyd and their song 'Peaches' for the credits, because they'd appeared on *RPM* several times and I knew the music backwards and loved it. It was edgy and slightly dangerous, something I thought fitted the personality of Floyd to perfection. Years later, towards the end of our working relationship, Floyd told me he used to let Hugh Cornwell, the lead singer and writer of their songs, play in his restaurant when he was a student at Bristol University. I thought it most odd that he had never thought to mention it at the time, because, being superstitious, if I'd known that in the beginning, I would have regarded it as a sign of good fortune.

I must also confess to an embarrassing Stranglers interlude that is right up there with the story of the guy who turned down the Beatles at Decca Records because, he said, guitar groups were on the way out. A year or so before I had moved to Plymouth I received a phone call from Hugh Cornwell to ask whether I'd be interested in listening to a new track they'd just recorded at the Crescent Studios in Bath. They wanted my opinion on which should be the 'A' side. I drove over there with Steve Poole, who directed all the music for the programmes, and unlike me was cool. The song was called 'Golden Brown' but for all Steve's cool, neither of us could understand a word of the lyrics. Perhaps it was a song about meeting a nicely tanned girl on holiday and having a lovely time, I thought.

'I like the tune very much,' I said, trying to sound positive and helpful. 'But the whole thing lacks the urgency and the strength of your earlier work, like "No More Heroes", "Hanging Around", and "Duchess". It sounds, and please don't take this the wrong way, as if you've gone a bit soft.'

Steve and I both agreed, 'It just isn't going to be a hit. Sorry about that.'

Now no matter where I go, all over the world from the Greek Islands to Japan, that huge bestseller of a song follows me like a spectre and whenever I hear it playing in a bar or restaurant or taxi, I hear those pathetic words 'It just isn't going to be a hit.'

When the very first programme of *Floyd on Fish* was completed, topped and tailed with the Stranglers' earlier work, I asked my line manager, my immediate boss Mike Read, to have a look at it. He'd always given me the freedom to do things that interested me, even though he did draw the line once on a series about witchcraft. I also knew he'd had to work overtime on my behalf to help me with all the stuff I simply didn't understand about managing my small department. I loved going out on 'recces', I loved filming and being in the cutting room. I even quite liked writing 'treatments' – the story outlines for new programmes. But I hated having to deal with things like finances, rostering and scheduling, and annual reports. I never really saw myself as a Boss, still don't, though I suppose I have got the hang of it a bit more over the last twenty-five years. The truth is, I just want to be out making films on the sea, on the moors, from Plymouth to Hong Kong, anywhere, frankly, but in an office, poring over some chart.

Viewing is a terribly painful process, as I've explained. However, Mike did laugh in all the right places. After the programme ended and the lights went on, though, he looked worried. Obviously he'd heard rumours floating around the building – aired mainly by the news staff, I may add – that Floyd was a little too fond of his glass of wine. At the time I regarded the news journalists as the playground bullies in our compact world of regional broadcasting in Plymouth. In the features department we would make programmes on artists, writers, musicians – sissy stuff really in comparison to the meat and potatoes of news – and rightly or wrongly, I was convinced that these bastards were trying to put the boot in by implying that Floyd was inebriated on camera. This was pretty ironic, I thought, as I had often watched many of them negotiate with some dismay the relatively short distance from the BBC club to the open doors of an awaiting taxi.

Mike wanted my reassurance that Floyd wasn't, at any time during the filming, 'pissed out of his head' as he so delicately put it.

'What?' I said, trying not to laugh. 'He's not pissed. He's just happy cooking things on the telly. He's a bit like Dean Martin without the singing. He uses the wine glass as a prop.' (Maybe Dean Martin wasn't a terribly helpful analogy.) 'He has the occasional slurp,' I went on, 'but he's certainly not drunk. Not by any stretch of the imagination.'

For a moment I thought he was going to ask me to sign an affidavit. I don't think I convinced him, and I certainly didn't tell him about the whiskies, or 'gold watches', as Floyd called them, that he'd consume before filming started.

It is images such as Floyd and his wine glass that help create a persona in the public's mind. Would Gordon (Ramsay) be as popular if he didn't use derivations of the word 'fuck' from time to time? Would we have taken so much notice of Gary (Rhodes) if he hadn't had unfeasibly spiky hair? If Nigella's bosom hadn't been quite as generous, might that have affected her viewing figures? And if the two ladies who rode motorcycle and pillion were of medium build, their popularity may not have been so instant. Even the hirsute motorcyclists who cook on camping stoves in the outdoors may have found themselves unknown without their beards and bikes. So maybe Floyd, without his glass of wine, may have disappeared from the world of British television. The fact is, it was never an intentional decision on my part to have him quaffing a glass or two while cooking. It was just something he did naturally.

Would we get away with it today? I don't think so. The world has definitely changed since those carefree days of the early Eighties. Half the nation drinks far too much; children as young as twelve are coming back from school blind drunk and the middle classes are shifting the

Sauvignon Blanc and Merlot like there's no tomorrow. So, no, we wouldn't get away with it today. But it never was about Floyd getting drunk on camera. The glass of wine was a symbol of being carefree. The message it gave to his viewers was this: cooking is great fun, it's not a drudge; it should be enjoyed to the full. What the wine glass represented, if you like, was an abandonment of weights, scales, measures, teaspoons, and dishes that had been cooked earlier. The wine glass said, 'Come on, just chop up a few cloves of garlic – it doesn't matter if it's three or four cloves, it could be five or six, or if you really like garlic, put in ten.'

After the first programme the *Western Morning News* started their review by saying 'Last night a star was born!' The fan letters began to arrive at the BBC by the sack-load and I went to Bristol to see Keith. I was overjoyed with the success of the series and I wanted to discuss what we might do next. But Keith didn't look like a man who had just presented a show that people seemed to love. He looked decidedly grumpy. It seemed his friends in Bristol couldn't see the programme because the regional transmission ended somewhere in the middle of the Somerset Levels. Even his mother couldn't see it in Wiveliscombe; such were the configurations of the various transmitters in the country that when she was expecting to see her beloved son, she probably got a programme from Cardiff on Welsh poetry. Keith might well be a star in Devon and Cornwall, but he was totally anonymous elsewhere in the country. As he so succinctly put it, he was bigger than Wham in Brixham and there was an article about him in the *Trout Farmers Weekly*, but it was hardly enough to persuade the maître d' at The Ivy to welcome him like an old friend.

If you don't get this series on the network, David, I'm going to come down to Plymouth and shoot you!

I'm pretty sure Keith was joking when he said these words but they did have a desperate ring to them. His restaurant had closed and it sounded like he owed quite a bit of cash to a number of people, including Her Majesty's Customs and Excise. I'd already told him I wanted to make another series and had just given him an advance on his fee. It had been no mean feat to persuade the BBC to part with the modest sum.

The problem, as he pointed out, was that he'd never be famous or get rich while the shows were airing only in the south-west of the country. This was a thorny issue, because the nature of regional broadcasting is that it is primarily a public service, and your first priority is to serve the region where you are based. However, the producers in Plymouth had a good track record of serving both the region *and* the network with excellent award-winning films. But they were mainly about wildlife and Floyd was an entirely different proposition. Unbeknown to Keith I'd had some depressing news from an insider in the scheduling department at BBC2, who had told me, in no uncertain terms, that Floyd was too much of a risk, mainly because he always had a glass of wine in his hand. What's more, I had had a difficult conversation with another high-flyer in the BBC, Terry Dobson, who told me that he didn't want me to be making cooking programmes, even on a local basis. I assured him as best I could that I wasn't making a cookery programme, but a series about a wasted resource (I was talking about fish, not Floyd), but he didn't seem convinced. I think he ended the conversation, rather like a TV detective inspector to a suspect, with 'I'm watching you, sonny.'

Undeterred, I had already started work with Keith on another local food series, which we were calling simply *Floyd on Food*. I thought we'd spread our wings and go to the island of Jersey, famous for its conger eel and marigold petal stew and its early new potatoes, Jersey Royals. We had arranged to create a lunch in a potato field for the head of agriculture there, a senator in the island's parliament. Earlier in the week Floyd had decided he wanted to cook calves' liver with a creamy mustard sauce and a hint of Calvados, accompanied by the celebrated Jersey Royals.

The location was beautiful, with its potato fields stretching right down to the sea, and it seemed to me to be a perfectly correct and natural thing to cook the produce in the exact location where it was grown. This scenario happens a great deal on television today, but twenty-five years ago, rather like cooking fish on a trawler in a force-eight gale, it was considered quite new and daring.

In the far distance there was a castle looming over a small harbour and beyond that a turquoise sea and white sand. It was a stunning spot, perfect for filming, and although it was March the weather was gloriously hot. We busied ourselves setting up the camping table, making sure we had enough gas and running through all the usual checks and balances for the filming, when it struck me like a thunderbolt. I'd bought the calves' liver in the market in St Helier and put it in the glove compartment of the hire car. Unfortunately, that was on Thursday morning and now it was Sunday afternoon and bloody hot. And, to make matters worse, this man in an immaculate white suit, striding purposefully towards us, looking every inch like the man from Del Monte, was none other than the senator himself – right on cue to get a serious bout of food poisoning.

I ran back across the dusty furrows to the lane where our cars were parked and braced myself for the moment of truth. It was baking inside the car, but I couldn't smell anything untoward. I opened the glove compartment and there, wrapped up in a carrier bag, was the senator's lunch. With trepidation I opened the bag and the smell of rancid, rotting offal hit me straight away; it was worse than cockles left in a warm room for a week, if not quite as bad as ragworms wrapped in newspaper and forgotten about for a fortnight in the boot of a car. I could see Floyd was waving and calling for me to come back and get the cooking started.

Today, of course, if I was faced with this problem, I would make a phone call to a well-chosen local hotel or restaurant and all would hopefully be solved. But here we were, early in the season, on a Sunday, when most places were closed. I couldn't think of a way out of it other than to confess to Keith.

Surprisingly, he was very understanding. He's very good in a moment of crisis; probably to do with his training as a lieutenant in the Tank Regiment.

'Well,' he said, 'it looks all right, it's nearly the right colour and if I keep it at arm's length and give it a good dousing in Calvados to get rid of the stench, it'll be fine for the cooking sequence. Just make sure you tell the senator to stick to the potatoes and don't touch the liver under any circumstances!'

What is a script?

We'd been filming for some time when Floyd said one morning, 'Do you think we should have a script?'

'A script?' I said, as astounded as if he had asked, 'Do you fancy going teetotal for the next six months?'

Keith explained that he'd met someone in television who said that presenters usually had scripts. So, indeed, if that were the case, where was his script? I could see his point of view, but the thought of writing a script had never crossed my mind. I explained to him in the nicest possible way that the idea was impractical for a number of very important reasons. The first was that we didn't seem to know what we were going to do until we got to our location; the second was that when we got there we made it up as we went along; and the third was that it would, I was sure, take all the fun out of filming. Also, and I didn't raise this point then, it sounded like a lot of hard work. So, in all the years we worked together that was the only conversation we ever had about writing a script.

Over the next few weeks we filmed on many boats, caught a great many fish and had a better time than on any holiday I'd ever been on. The days seemed frustratingly short, but that might have been because on certain occasions the lunches could be extraordinarily long. In the absence of a script we'd hatch ideas over lunch or dinner the night before filming, and we'd developed a habit of 'going for a walk in the garden' just before the cameras turned over, when we'd have a chat about roughly the way the sequence might go. That was as close as we came to planning. We were on a big culinary adventure, and we knew roughly where we might start, but we never really knew where we would end up.

I was learning a great deal about food and wine from this very debonair and funny man, who could be exceptionally good company and who never seemed afraid of any challenge I put in front of him. There were times when I was scared out of my wits in a boat in a howling gale, hanging on with white knuckles to any piece of marine plywood or steel hawser that would take my weight, but Keith would nonchalantly light a cigarette and take a pull from his hip flask with all the cares of someone having a chat in the saloon bar of his local pub.

Floyd may have had his faults but cowardice certainly wasn't one of them. Once, much later, he rescued me from a brothel in Malaga. We had blundered in thinking it was a rather degenerate-looking bar, the sort of place where writers and artists would go in the Thirties. Keith had nipped out to buy cigarettes, and while he was away a couple of ladies joined me at the bar and struck up a conversation. They heard my accent and, for some reason, kept asking me if I was from Portsmouth. I bought them both a drink, hoping that Floyd would come back any minute. Just as I was halfway through telling the women about Admiral Nelson and the Battle of Trafalgar he returned, saying his chauffeur would help us to find a better bar than this one. I asked for the bill, and when the barman told me it was nearly 7,000 pesetas I nearly fell off my bar stool. I only had 500 on me.

'Two beers and two fruit cocktails. How could that add up to 7,000 pesetas?' Floyd demanded.

'The women,' said the barman. 'Your frien' speak to the women for nearly an hour – so you pay up.'

Floyd searched his pockets, all the while giving me one of his best withering looks.

'I've only got a thousand, and this idiot here has only got 500,' he said, squaring up to the barman, who by now was flanked by a couple of menacing-looking friends.

Floyd, like Michael Caine facing the hordes of Zulus for the first time (*Zulu* was Keith's favourite film), told them, 'We're leaving now, and you'll have to fight the two of us to stop us from reaching those doors.'

Steady on, I thought, but Keith was unstoppable. We made it to the door and his limo was waiting right outside.

'Get in you tosser,' he said, before the door closed with an expensive and very reassuring clunk.

I still felt pretty intimidated whenever we found ourselves in posh restaurants with thick carpets, surrounded by hushed murmurings and snooty maître d's. On one occasion Keith and I were in such a restaurant in Paris. The menu was so elaborate, I couldn't understand half of it, but what I could comprehend contained amazingly complex dishes with ingredients like turbot and foie gras.

When the very condescending waiter came over and asked, 'Monsieur. You are ready to order?' Floyd looked up and said, 'Egg and chips please.'

I looked at him in total amazement, thinking he was joking. But he wasn't. 'I'll have the same,' I said.

The waiter didn't bat an eyelid. Out came wonderful eggs and chips perfectly cooked in goose fat. It was brilliant. I had to take my hat off to Floyd. What balls; what style.

One day we had a break in filming and it was time to go back to the office, which turned out to be extremely fortuitous. We were about to be visited by Brian Wenham, who had previously been the controller of BBC2, and now had an even more important role in charge of all programming for the entire television service. We didn't get many visits from the top brass and so we were all very excited to see someone from London. The boardroom was set for lunch, with our finest cutlery and bottles of wine. Jim Dickman, our commissionaire, who used to be a stoker on the Arctic convoys during the last war, was all set to serve the drinks in his finest bib and tucker.

At first sight I thought Mr Wenham looked very much like the actor Claude Rains who played the suave but corrupt Vichy French police officer in the classic film, *Casablanca*. He didn't take very long to drink his Scotch and he seemed utterly affable and relaxed with everyone in the room. This was in the days when BBC bosses liked a drink. Nowadays their counterparts guzzle mineral water, and although most of them look like they should be head of the sixth form, they generally have a gloomy disposition and all seem to ride bicycles.

Brian Wenham was a master at working a room. Everyone he spoke to seemed to beam within a few seconds. Like most organizations the BBC has its fair share of creeps who laugh at all the boss's jokes even though the punchline might well be in Swahili – but this wasn't like that. Brian Wenham radiated real warmth and it was obvious that he had a great love for the television business. It was like watching someone go round a room switching on all the lights.

Over lunch of roast lamb and Cornish new potatoes, cooked as always by the excellent Mrs Boggis, the much feared and admired head of the canteen, he asked if he could see a handful of programmes, just three or four, the sort of stuff that was representative of the station. This was a golden opportunity, not to be missed, to show *Floyd on Fish*.

The rather grand Victorian staircase that led up to my office always made me think of Hitchcock's film *Rebecca*, the scene where Max's poor timid wife dares to put on a dress that used to be worn by his ravishing, but very dead wife. I remember thinking, as I walked up it, that I had a real dilemma here. On the one hand this was my chance to show this emperor penguin what we sand fleas could do in the regions on tight budgets, and if I was truly honourable what I should show him was a selection of my colleagues' best work. On the other hand, and in my defence, Mr Wenham struck me as the sort of person who might get bored easily and would therefore be most interested in the first thing he saw. I saw the moment as a God sent opportunity to show him my programme, and put aside my few pangs of guilt. Minutes later, the Stranglers' 'Waltz in Black' was booming out of the television set, accompanying the opening montage of shots of a bedraggled Keith Floyd sipping a glass of wine while bobbing around on a variety of fishing boats.

It turned out my hunch was quite right about this particular emperor penguin's short attention span. After watching for five minutes or so he asked, 'Is he pissed?'

'No,' I said, 'he's just happy to be a cook on the telly. He's a bit like Dean Martin but he cooks things instead of singing songs.'

I gave him copies of all the programmes we had made, and a month or so later *Floyd on Fish* was on the network, and Keith was basking in the warmth of new found success. And, to a minor degree, so was I.

Suddenly Keith was being recognized by total strangers in London and all over the country. Even the great gourmet and food critic of the time, Egon Ronay, phoned up to ask me what the viewing figures were for the series. His voice sounded like the soundtrack to a bad British espionage film, and at first I thought it was my good friend and fellow director, Bernard Hall, putting on his German spy's accent. Actually, I didn't know how many people watched Floyd's debut and frankly I didn't care. I was just so pleased that it had been shown to a wider audience. Today every producer I meet seems to be concerned about one thing: viewing figures. But once upon a time in Plymouth statistics didn't come into it. It was far more important to have a glowing review from an important TV critic like Nancy Banks-Smith or Clive James. I'd hear Floyd's voice on the radio and read about his exploits in the newspapers. He was becoming a highly desirable commodity and clearly enjoying this new celebrity. And good luck to him.

PART V

Early rumblings

My friends who work in the television industry consider me lazy and indulgent – I know this because they tell me so quite often, especially when they've had a few drinks. They, on the other hand, prefer to make documentary films on far more gritty matters than seafood paellas and fish soup. I am regularly accused of paddling around in the warm, shallow end of the programme-making pool, when I should actually be involved in things that really matter in society, such as drugs, racism, existence on sink estates, and all of life's dreadful inequalities. But from my experience a diehard documentary-maker is someone who has a real understanding of social politics – something I've never really got to grips with. I did once make a film about the whys and wherefores of being a skinhead on the Scotswood Road in Newcastle. They were a pretty notorious bunch at the time – though surprisingly friendly towards me – and I was trying to work out why they did what they did, but after spending six weeks with them, I was none the wiser.

As a young film editor I spent many a joyous lunchtime and the occasional evening in smoky Tyneside pubs with Marxist journalists, lefty songwriters and film-makers. I had come to Newcastle because I knew by now that I wanted to be a film editor at the BBC, and there were no vacancies in the south of England. So I packed a suitcase and waved goodbye to my mother and my job at Southern Television, where, by now, I had graduated to the dizzy heights of Assistant Film Editor, somewhat nearer to the job description I had applied for in the first place. I drove the 280 miles north from Southampton in my Austin Healey Sprite, which was third-hand and falling to bits, but I loved it. Newcastle upon Tyne in the late Sixties was everything I thought and feared it would be, having never been north of Winchester before. I'd read a number of novels about the north, well two really – *Room at the Top* and *A Kind of Loving*. I'd watched *Coronation Street* and seen the film *This Sporting Life* and all of these fired my imagination. For some reason I had the impression, largely from reading John Braine's novel, and also being an eternal optimist, that people were having more sex up north than in the south.

The first thing I noticed coming over the Tyne Bridge on a cold winter's morning was the smell of beer coming from the chimneys of the Federation Brewery. It would hang over the coaly Tyne like a benign steamy cloud smelling of hops and malted barley. I'd like to think that when Alan Hull wrote the Tyneside anthem, 'Fog on the Tyne', he had this delicious aroma in his thoughts.

The next thing I noticed were the buildings. The banks, offices and department stores were as fine architecture as I'd ever set eyes on; as impressive as London, and streets ahead of Southampton, but they looked as if they had been carved out of ebony. A century of soot from the factories, steam trains, and shipyards up and down the Tyne had gradually painted them black. Then there were the pubs: great Victorian gin palaces, their rococo ceilings stained brown with smoke from a billion Woodbines. In 1968 no women were allowed in the public bar of The Grapes, the pub that we frequented. The bar would be packed three-deep with men, dressed, it seemed to me at the time, identically in flat caps and fawn raincoats and carrying army issue knapsacks. This was drinking with real intensity. Pint after pint would be consumed, with little conversation, in the hour or so between the factory whistle blowing at the end of the shift and the buses leaving from the Haymarket to take the men home along the banks of the Tyne or over the bridge to Gateshead. The men made me think of a group of paratroopers waiting for the green light that signalled the jump. This was a moment of peace before the bus ride home to the wife and kids.

It was in one of these pubs, The Portland, that I would sit listening to my new extremely articulate friends talking politics and art. They seemed to know so much about things that had never crossed my mind before: percentages of government expenditure for this and that, Polaris missiles, South African apples, unemployment figures, Vietnam and Leonard Cohen. Then, of course, there were the riots in Paris and Grosvenor Square. It was as if a flame had been lit and the petrol bombs being aimed with frightening accuracy at the French riot police were igniting radical thoughts all over the Western world. The Rolling Stones were even inspired to write 'Street Fighting Man'.

At first I hardly made any contribution of value to the conversation – no one seemed particularly interested in fishing, sports cars, and camping. On one occasion Alan Hull, the lead singer from the band Lindisfarne, who was a regular member of our group, asked me what my favourite film was. I knew that the mention of James Bond brought snarls of derision, so I thought about it for some time and finally said *The Sound of Music*. Everybody started laughing so much they nearly choked. Some of them looked as if they were crying. I should have said Roman Polanski's *Knife in the Water* or *Citizen Kane*, which most people chose, but I hadn't seen either. It was lucky I hadn't mentioned *Bambi*, a film that made me cry so much when I was about ten that I had to be taken out of the cinema.

I'd love to be like them, I thought: to be considered a left-wing radical; to be able to talk about Pinter, Brecht, and Beckett without drawing breath; to have read Foucault and Sartre and to smile with an inner understanding while listening to Leonard Cohen late at night, trying to impress some girl over a cup of Nescafé.

In Newcastle I met Bernard Hall, also a film editor, who became my best friend. Bernard used to hold court and keep people enthralled. He used words like 'dichotomy', 'polemic', 'didactic', and 'condone'. He had a public school accent and became extremely angry when it came to the injustices of modern life. He also had long hair, which helps put across radical thoughts very well. Unfortunately, I was starting to go bald. He suggested it would be a good idea if I read the *Guardian* for a week or two before joining in the conversation. He also suggested

I carried a rolled-up copy of it into the pub, because it would make me seem much more intelligent. According to Bernard, reading the *Guardian* was essential, the key to getting on in the media in the north-east – nearly as important as being a card-carrying member of the Labour Party. I followed his advice, but after a week I found the *Guardian* incredibly difficult and bought a donkey jacket, a red scarf and a pair of Clarks suede desert boots instead.

We drank Exhibition Ale, the best beer on Tyneside, and ate the only food to be had in those days in most of the pubs: huge baps – stottie cakes they called them – unbuttered and the size of farmers' caps, filled with hunks of Scottish red Cheddar and thick slices of raw onion. They made your eyes water, but they went so well with the beer. Sometimes, usually on a Monday lunchtime, the pubs would serve tattie pot, a kind of Geordie version of a Lancashire hotpot, using leftover lamb with black pudding, onions and potatoes cooked in stock. It was truly delicious and very cheap, a dish born out of the times when people were hard up, so it never went out of fashion on Tyneside, until the pizza arrived. It's also the sort of food I come across from time to time these days in restaurants where the chef has decided to give a traditional dish a facelift. So instead of the tattie pot arriving at your table in a sizzling coal black cast iron pot, it appears on a square white plate with turned up corners, a small island of golden potatoes and black pudding sitting in a pool of tepid redcurrant coulis, with a forlorn sprig of rosemary sticking out of the top. I always think these kinds of 'reinventions' are a bit like taking a muddy, hard-working sheepdog to a fancy poodle parlour.

It was in Newcastle that my great love affair with food really started. For several months I lived in a bedsit in Heaton, then an unfashionable suburb of Newcastle. It was very clean and tidy and it had a Baby Belling cooker. Inside it I found one of the most useful cookery books ever written, *Cooking in a Bedsitter*, by Katharine Whitehorn. It was simplicity itself and funny too.

The centre of Newcastle was blessed with a wonderful Victorian market, called the Grainger after the famous architect who designed much of this city's fine architecture. I'd never seen anything like it before. It was like a massive, ornate railway station, with high vaulted ceilings and it was chock full of life and colour. I was sure such places simply didn't exist in the south; maybe they'd all been bombed during the last war. It even had a tiny Marks & Spencer, which was one of the first penny bazaars in the country. It's amazing to think this is how it started, with Mr Marks and Mr Spencer peddling goods in their shop for a penny, when now they sell everything from shoes and Champagne to 'Achaari chicken with carrot and mung bean curry, tenderstem broccoli, spiced basmati rice and a cumin and coriander raita'. The store still displayed the old sign from a hundred years ago, which said, 'Don't ask the price it's a penny.' Except this was 1968 and the prices had gone up a bit.

I went to the market almost every day in my lunch hour to buy ingredients to bring Miss Whitehorn's recipes to life. On one side of the market there was an area set aside for shoppers to have something to eat and a cup of tea. I'd always, if I had the time, have a saveloy dip. I was told by the nice old lady who served them that this was Tyneside's most famous dish: a spicy red sausage served in a roll with hot pease pudding. Nowhere in the whole of the country is this pudding, made from boiled dried peas, so revered. The lady at the market didn't know why the saveloy had made its mark with Tynesiders, but with the benefit of making a couple of hundred programmes on food behind me, I wouldn't mind betting it was introduced by Italian craftsmen: the sculptors, stonemasons and artists who came to our towns in Victorian times to decorate the new civic buildings and churches. A similar thing happened on the other side of the Pennines in the seventeenth century, when German lead workers started to make their own sausage in exactly the same way they did back at home, with pure pork, without rusk or breadcrumbs, hung from hooks around the room, in one long tube to dry. We know it today as the Cumberland sausage.

The Baby Belling and I started our gastronomic journey together – nothing fancy, there'd be plenty of time for all that later. A simple stew was the first thing I cooked and it was so disappointing because the meat was tough, the carrots hard and the stock watery. This wasn't the fault of the recipe. The problem was that the temptation to go to the pub after work with my new found friends was so strong that sometimes I didn't begin to cook until nearly ten o'clock at night, so I was nearly passing out with hunger pangs and I found it impossible to wait for the allotted number of hours to pass before tucking in.

Weekends were a different matter, with plenty of time to shop and to prepare. The first real, grown-up dish I cooked from Miss Whitehorn's book was beef stroganoff. I'd never heard of it before, let alone eaten fillet steak or soured cream and it sounded so posh. It was the sort of dish I could imagine being served at some glamorous restaurant under great silver domes by waiters dressed as Cossacks. If it hadn't been to do with the attraction of the opposite sex, and one particular girl who worked for the BBC, then I would have quite happily cooked stewed mince with onions and carrots with an Oxo cube à la Katie from the TV ad, but I was expecting none other than the boss's secretary, and an invitation to a bedsit for some stewed mince didn't have quite the right ring to it.

For the first time in that humble abode I started to cook when I was sober. I discovered what an easy and enjoyable thing it was to do. I sliced the onions and the green peppers. I'd like to apologize at this point to Katharine Whitehorn and Monsieur Stroganoff, just in case there wasn't a green pepper involved in the original recipe. I think it was a case of overenthusiastic shopping on my part and the inclusion of green peppers made the dish seem even more tantalizing and foreign. The aroma of the peppers, once the knife had cut through them, was completely new to me. It had a fruity, peppery freshness, like the smell of wet trees after the rain. Cooks today look down their noses at the poor green pepper, but back in the Sixties they were 'exotic', just as the furniture of the time was 'contemporary'.

I was desperate to cook this dish well because I fear I had presented the invitation to the young woman in a dastardly underhand way. Her name was Elaine and she was as fair of face and body as you could ever wish to find, with a lovely outgoing personality and, on top of that, she liked a pint or two. She was in every way quite perfect. But I may have given her the impression that I was a bit of a gourmet. I'd never seen the likes of an avocado or tasted an aubergine, but through the power of these two words 'beef stroganoff' I had enticed this delightful girl back to my humble room. Now all I had to do was to cook the bloody thing without cocking it up.

Apparently the whole point of stroganoff is that you must cook the fillet steak rare, which means that it is a relatively quick assembly job once all the sautéing has been completed. As expertly as I could I tipped all the sautéed vegetables into a saucepan. Elaine had arrived and was sitting in the one and only chair, watching with polite interest as I gave a sort of running commentary while I cooked. I thought it would be a cool thing to have a glass of Mateus Rosé, the only wine, apart from Rocamar and Hirondelle, which I'd heard of. Because I was flying solo I'd hidden Katharine Whitehorn away in a cupboard, and was trying to remember the cooking process as best I could. I thought I'd model myself on Michael Caine from *The Ipcress File*, a man who could expertly rustle up a Spanish omelette in a few minutes, while making highly successful sensual overtures to his attractive dinner guest at the same time. Unfortunately, Elaine had never seen *The Ipcress File*.

I quickly fried the pieces of fillet steak in butter, looking, I hoped, as if I'd done this a million times before, and then tipped them into the saucepan with the lightly fried vegetables. This was completely the wrong way to go about it as I found out later; the ingredients should have been poured over the steak. Elaine, I sensed, was impressed with my efforts. With a flourish I poured in the soured cream and stirred it so it heated gently. Finally I produced my plastic Jif lemon and added a few squirts to the saucepan. *Voilà!*

Surprisingly, it was good. So good in fact that we got engaged shortly afterwards and went on camping holidays in the Lake District, where we drank pints of Jennings Bitter in lovely pubs and afterwards made our way back to our little tent where, on a primus stove, I would cook mince with carrots, onions and an Oxo cube.

Bungalow days

John Craven was a regional journalist in Newcastle at the time, and we became friends. He had an old, slightly dilapidated bungalow on the outskirts of Newcastle and we decided it would be good fun if I gave up the bedsit and shared with him. A few weeks later Bernard Hall joined us, followed by Tony Bannister, a graphic artist who also worked at the BBC. This meant I could start to cook in a full-sized oven for a captive audience. I started to make stews with all those fresh and attractive ingredients from Grainger Market: steak and kidney, carrots, turnips, leeks, and potatoes, and, of course, a couple of Oxo stock cubes. It was good, hearty, wholesome, and tasty fare, and I particularly liked the way the potatoes would break down in the cooking and thicken the stew. As the week went on, I would keep replenishing the large saucepan with new ingredients, so one pot could stretch to meals for days.

One evening I overheard a snatched conversation between John and Bernard, discussing the merits of my cooking. The words 'fucking stew again' came up. This was quite contrary to the enthusiastic reception I had received the first time I had cooked this dish several weeks ago. Now they openly proclaimed my cooking bland and boring, which I found rather hurtful. On one occasion I had admittedly caught Bernard adding a bottle of red wine to the saucepan.

'This is an English stew,' I had said, highly affronted. 'If I wanted a fucking beef bourguignon I'd have used garlic and herbs and maybe a pig's trotter and some brandy. But this is a taste of England.'

'Well, can you do a taste of France sometime soon, because we're all getting fed up with this night after night,' was the answer.

At their accusation of bland and boring I was tempted to tell them all to go back to their tinned Fray Bentos steak and kidney pies, which used to erupt like Vesuvius all over the oven because they failed to read the instructions about piercing the lid before cooking. Instead, I decided to become slightly more adventurous, trying my hand at risotto, spaghetti bolognese (by now it was 1969, and everybody was making spaghetti bolognese) and seafood paella. John Craven and I went on a lads' package holiday to Spain, and apart from sangria and sunstroke my abiding memory of a fortnight on the Costa Brava was paella. Back home again in Newcastle I bought fresh prawns, mussels and squid, along with saffron and garlic, and prepared it to cookery book perfection. The rice was golden, the way it should be, dotted with pink prawns, squid and peas, and I left it to absorb all of the stock. But when I went back into the kitchen to check on it everything had turned black. Bernard had thought it a really good idea to put the ink from the squid into the finished dish. I'd spent all day buying the ingredients and preparing this masterpiece for some Visigoth to come along and turn it black as coal.

'They have black paellas all over Spain,' insisted Bernard, trying to make out he had done me an enormous favour.

'No they don't. They have black risotto in Italy but all the paellas in Spain are golden. That's why they use fucking saffron ... which costs a bomb.' And with that I stormed out.

Apparently the paella was delicious despite the colour, but just wait, I thought, until the next time Bernard is doing the cooking.

Those bungalow days were wonderful fun and the culinary arguments made life even more enjoyable. But after a few months it was time for me to get married. Even on the way to the church I told John, who was my best man, that I was making a dreadful mistake.

'It's a bit late now, David,' he said, sounding very much like Alan Bennett, with his sensible Yorkshire accent. 'She's a lovely girl and you're very lucky.'

This was so true; but I was having such a fine time at the bungalow and I didn't want it to stop.

We had a short honeymoon, a driving holiday in Northern Ireland in my second-hand MGB. Every bridge we drove over I'd get my rod out of the boot and try to catch a fish. I must have stopped a couple of dozen times on our journey without the slightest whiff of a fish. Elaine was extremely patient and we were getting on very well though I could sense she was starting to get just a little bored watching me cast a spinner, an artificial metal fish, in every stream, river and lake we came across. And then the impossible happened. A salmon – a huge one – took the bait. I could see the bright silver flash of its flanks in the peaty water as it fought to free itself from the hook. I looked for Elaine to share this momentous piscatorial adventure, but it had started to drizzle and she was inside the car reading a book.

The rod, a light split cane affair, was bending alarmingly now as the fish desperately tried to make a break for it downstream. If I tried to stop him my line would break, so I'd have to go downstream with him. I climbed off the bridge over a low fence and managed to squeeze through some elderberry bushes. I nearly snapped the line, but the fish had stopped running and seemed to be resting in a pool, which, luckily for me, had a small beach on my side of the river. I didn't have a landing net, so this area of stones and pebbles would be perfect for bringing this fine specimen to the shore. Oh how I wished Elaine could see me looking every inch the fisherman. Funny that she should have chosen to go off and read in the car, because when we started the honeymoon five days ago she was very interested in my little fishing escapades. She'd want to know all about the various baits and artificial lures and the best places along the riverbank to cast a line. She even wanted to have a go herself. I even let her have a few casts, but she managed to get the line mangled up inside the fixed spool reel when she was reeling in, and it took me ages to untangle it.

I'd read somewhere in a favourite old book of mine, written by a man who called himself BB, that all the fishing in Ireland was free. It was written shortly after the First World War and it said that apparently you could fish anywhere you wanted to. How good it felt to land a fish without having to scour the horizon for fear of water bailiffs. It didn't occur to me that fifty years on things might have changed.

It was as if my salmon knew his time had come. He didn't want to fight very much and so it was a pretty easy job to entice him into the shallow water, even with light tackle. This was the biggest fish I'd ever caught in my life, nearly three feet long, gasping his last on the pebbles in front of me. I felt so sorry for him, I decided to let him go. I could just imagine the conversation with Elaine as I returned to the car, with no fish, but a great tale.

'How big?' she would say.

But sadly my fish had swallowed the lure. It was so deep in his gullet that I had no choice but to put him quickly out of his misery. I wished I hadn't caught him.

These were the days, before large-scale salmon farming, when fresh salmon was considered quite a luxury and I couldn't let a lovely fish go to waste, so when we returned to the hotel, I asked the owner if he would like to buy a fresh-run salmon to put on the menu that evening. The response was quite alarming. The Irish sense of humour which had been so evident on our arrival completely escaped him. Apparently the salmon season had finished several weeks earlier and anyone caught landing such a fish was likely to be given a hefty fine, especially if they were trying to sell it. Oh dear. I thought about burying it, but I couldn't do that to such a beautiful fish.

Because it had rained so much, we had decided to cut the honeymoon short, so the next day we caught the ferry from Larne across the Irish Sea then drove to our new home near Durham, and the salmon came too. It was far too big to fit into our largest saucepan, so we shared it with our new next-door neighbours, Alan and Dorothy. Even so, for days to come we were still dining on salmon, until we were heartily sick of it. Many years later I read that in the days before the Industrial Revolution when the Tyne ran pure and the salmon were plentiful, apprentices in Newcastle had written into their contracts of employment that they wouldn't be fed salmon more than three times a week. I knew how they felt. Even today I prefer tinned wild red salmon, especially in an old-fashioned English salad with lettuce, cucumber, spring onions, boiled eggs, salad cream, and new potatoes. Of course, I take great relish in telling Rick Stein this, because Rick thinks my devotion to good old-fashioned British food, from lamb chops to tinned salmon, makes me some kind of culinary dinosaur.

He raises an eyebrow and says, 'David, have you tried eating fresh salmon again …' It's one of the many things on which we beg to differ, although I suspect, secretly, he knows I'm right.

PART VI

Lost in France

France was the big love of Floyd's life and Provence held a special place in his heart, so we simply had to go. I'd love to say that I painstakingly sweated for weeks at a time over every nuance of French regional food before submitting the idea for our new series to a higher authority. But I found a really good book on French food for half price at Taunton Deane services, copied all the best bits on to a couple of pages of A4, called it *Floyd on France* and sent it off to London – and that was it.

I think what clinched it for us was that BBC Books said they'd be jolly keen to invest in such a project, which meant that if Keith wrote a book to accompany the series, the television service got it cheaply. The book subsidy meant that my filming budget went suddenly from a miserly £2,000 per programme up to a handsome £10,000. So, in 1986, after much preliminary research, we opened a map of France and had a chat about where to go. We headed off on a 'recce', searching for locations, characters, great cooks, and all the necessary ingredients needed to make a television programme which, hopefully, would give the viewer at home a real taste of France.

We started in the village of Trémolat in the Périgord region in the Dordogne valley, a gastronomically rich area known for its ducks, geese, walnuts, truffles, and all sorts of charcuterie. I had chosen the village of Trémolat quite by chance, because it had a beautiful campsite on the banks of the Dordogne where I planned to stay while Keith was booked into a rather nice hotel, Le Vieux Logis, on the outskirts of the village.

I found out later that one of my favourite film directors (after Hitchcock, of course), Claude Chabrol, had set his masterpiece *Le Boucher* in this very village – what luck. If it was good enough for him, it was certainly good enough for me. The film is a classic. In this idyllic village the headmistress, a beautiful chain-smoking young woman, makes friends with the local chain-smoking butcher. He clearly fancies her like mad because he's always giving her the choice cuts from his window – a leg of lamb, veal escalopes, and some lovely looking steak. Meanwhile, outside this tight-knit community, in the stunning countryside, there's a serial killer on the loose: gripping stuff. There's a powerful scene where the children go on a picnic under the limestone cliffs on the banks of the Dordogne. Slowly, almost imperceptibly at first, red spots of blood start to appear on the children's sandwiches signalling the demise of yet another beautiful woman, fallen victim to the butcher's knife. Chabrol's theme is the classic one of all time, that of a primeval beast lurking behind a thin veneer of bourgeois civilization, a kind of *Midsomer Murders* for *Guardian* readers. I think it's a shame they called it *Le Boucher* because you know who did it when you're queuing up to buy your ticket at the cinema. No one can accuse the French of being afraid of the painfully obvious.

I had decided to camp for a number of reasons. The first and most important one was that I enjoy camping. I love being under canvas and hearing the wind and the rain at night; and I adore cooking breakfast in the open air. It has to be bacon and eggs, though there lay a problem. How is it that even now, in this country that prides itself so much on its glorious food, they still haven't understood the joy of the noble rasher of bacon? Can you find such a thing in a local *boucherie*? I think not. Lardons, yes; proper rashers, no. Unless you ask the butcher to cut you a *barde de lard*, which is a thin piece of streaky bacon normally used to wrap around meat such as game.

My second reason for camping was that I thought it a good idea for Keith and me to have a little space from each other, especially in the evenings around dinner, always a potentially tricky time, as Keith was becoming exceedingly cross with my lack of French. The more glasses of wine he had the crosser he got, so it seemed safer to part company after pudding. Third, I was trying to save money.

It proved a good choice for Keith to stay at that hotel because the owner, Bernard, knew every local food producer of worth: fishermen, cheese-makers, vineyard owners, ham curers. He was a treasure trove of information which saved us days, if not weeks, of precious research time. I got the impression that Bernard thought I was Keith's servant, living in a tent by the river, while his lord and master had a suite and the use of a fine dining room. I don't think Keith did much to dispel that idea, since whenever I had dinner with them at the hotel he and Bernard would talk non-stop in spirited French, leaving me bored to distraction and longing to get back to my tent. I would have happily swapped all the science, algebra, technical drawing, religious studies, and the whole nine yards I had learnt at school, just to be able to make some basic conversation.

On our first morning after arriving we visited a goose farmer on his ramshackle old farm, where some of the buildings dated back to the fourteenth century. He was known locally for making exquisite pâté de foie gras – the best in the area. Keith and I had had some in the hotel the night before, and, though I hesitate to say so, knowing how much scorn and indignation is generated by this product, it was utterly delicious, a real taste of luxury; it was sweet, buttery and silky, and a great match with the local golden dessert wine, Monbazillac.

I was dreading seeing the grim business of force feeding geese in order to engorge their livers, making them six times their normal size. But instead of hundreds of depressed looking geese locked in cages on death row, there were about fifty large white birds queuing to be hand fed by the farmer's wife. She had a metal funnel, the tube of which she inserted down the long throats of the geese. It had a handle on the top and, I presume, some form of corkscrew mechanism inside which forced warm, softened sweetcorn kernels quickly down the gullets of the geese. The process took just a minute for each goose and all the time she was gently stroking the neck of the bird, helping the corn go down. The farmer only started this feeding process three weeks before the birds were killed and the geese were patiently waiting their turn, much like dairy cows queuing up outside a milking parlour.

After an hour or so it was time to go, because we had arranged to meet a freshwater fisherman, who went by the delightful name of Monsieur Le Pélican, in half an hour's time. Keith was just starting the car when the farmer took me aside and, from what I could gather, given that the only three words I understood were 'grandparents', 'honoured' and 'BBC', he said he would be honoured if we could meet his grandparents, who had started the business years ago. The French hold the BBC close to their hearts, and I thought maybe his grandparents were resistance fighters during the last war, who had listened to the BBC under the very noses of the Germans.

The rain had begun to beat a violent tattoo on the roof of the car, so I got in to explain this to Keith, but before I could do so, he started to drive off.

'Time for a coffee and a brandy. A quick heart starter before our next meeting,' he pronounced cheerily.

'Stop! We can't go yet. We've got to wait,' I protested as the farmer's Renault 16 went bouncing past us, through the muddy puddles on the way to the main road, presumably to fetch the grandparents.

'Why? We've said our goodbyes, so let's go!'

I explained the situation, but he wasn't happy. That warming brandy was beckoning.

We sat for ten minutes or so in silence, Keith smoking impatiently, until the rain stopped and I could escape from the smoke inside the car. I thought if I could split open a couple of herrings and hang them on the rear-view mirror they would be kippers by the time the farmer returned.

Another ten minutes went by and Keith wound down his window and said, 'How do you *know* he's gone to fetch his grandparents when you don't speak a word of French?'

I started to answer indignantly, when I saw the Renault turn into the farm track and start bouncing its way back towards us. I couldn't see any grandparents, only the farmer.

'Great,' came a voice from somewhere inside the smoky interior of the Volvo. 'He's gone all that fucking way and they were out. Maybe they've gone off to play bingo. Brilliant!'

The farmer parked the car and beckoned to us to come over. He opened the rear door and out flopped two huge but slightly doddery geese, the grandparents of the geese we'd seen earlier in the morning. Floyd turned up the collar of his trench coat and shot me the kind of look that Claude Chabrol might have spent a whole morning rehearsing to menacing perfection for *Le Boucher*, just before he put the knife into an *escalope de veau*.

A week in Provence

On the first day of the shoot proper, we found ourselves driving deep in the south of France among fields of sunflowers, with the top down, thinking about what to have for lunch.

134

Filming is so easy when you're surrounded by such beauty. I had never been to Provence before and it was the early morning light that I found so magical. It went from lavender to turquoise, then to apricot, before bathing all the fields, vineyards, and hilltop villages in pinky gold. I don't think that happens at home.

The first day's filming was a joy. Being a simple soul I tend to shoot scenes roughly in the order in which I imagine them to be shown in the programme. So, to introduce our intrepid presenter, expounding his sheer delight at being back in Provence, the first thing we did was borrow an old Citroën Mahari, which is a French version of our Mini Moke, and drive it up a mountain track with a sheer drop of hundreds of feet to one side. Against this romantic landscape, driving this underpowered and underwhelming piece of French engineering, Floyd, looking every inch like Mr Toad, rattled up the stony track leaving a cloud of dust in his wake, talking passionately to the camera's lens.

I was crushed up in the back against Timmy White, the sound recordist, while hanging on to Clive the cameraman, who was kneeling precariously on the front passenger seat, filming Floyd's piece to camera while trying not to fall out of the car. Clive is what people in Hollywood in the Fifties would have described as the strong silent type, while young Timmy was as gangly as a colt and full of good nature and enthusiasm. Together with the assistant cameraman, Andy MacCormack, who reminded me very much of a kind of hippy Irish wolfhound, all whiskery and lean, and Steve Williams, who did the lighting and got us into many an overbooked restaurant on account of his resemblance to Mick Jagger, they would be our trusty crew for many years to come.

TV audiences have become used to chefs linking sequences as they are driving along, and filming in the most unlikely places, but back then I think we all knew that apart from having lots of fun, we were breaking new ground.

'It's the light, the colours of the buildings, the markets with their lovely misshapen vegetables that really taste of something,' Floyd was saying. 'It's the people who really care about food – whoops, a bit too near the edge there – it's the great dishes of this place, made with garlic, saffron, wine and lemons, it's the local knowledge that goes right back to the days of the ancient Greeks ... that's why I'm so pleased to come back here. To me it's like coming home.'

Gosh, I thought, still clutching Clive, that was a tour de force, and it came straight from the heart. When Keith was good he was very, very good.

We centred our production on the beautiful town of L'Isle sur la Sorgue. The French call it the Venice of the South because of the beautiful little bridges that span the myriad of streams and canals flowing through and around the medieval centre. Here they have a vibrant Saturday market that is a film-maker's dream: old ladies sniffing and prodding melons to test for ripeness, and bad-tempered cheese-sellers saying, 'Fuck off with your camera, if you want to film me, you give me some money!'

Floyd, of course, was in his element because, years before, he had owned a successful little restaurant in the town and he knew many of the stallholders. Effortlessly, we shot a whole scene with the camera simply following Keith, like a faithful dog, from stall to stall through the busy, crowded market, buying the ingredients to make lunch for a dozen or so old friends. There were virulent purple bulbs of garlic, gnarled red peppers, dusty tomatoes of varying sizes still attached to the vine, neat bunches of white asparagus, and lampreys, gasping their last on the fishmonger's slab. Every time I was tempted to say 'cut' (reminding myself that each 400-foot roll of film cost over a hundred pounds and only lasted ten minutes) we would come to a stall full of hams, terrines, and sausages, or a mountain of olives, nuts, and preserved lemons. Now might be a good place to call 'cut' but no – not yet. Here were the stalls preparing the hot food – if only the camera could transmit the smells of huge paellas full of mussels, rabbit, and massive pink prawns still with their shells on, or the huge frying pan full of snails, looking like hundreds of shiny humbugs, or next door, the biggest rotisserie I'd ever set eyes on with thirty or so golden chickens basting the potatoes below with their life's juices. At last, hurray, we had reached the stalls of trainers and rucksacks. Now I could say 'cut'. Except Clive had already done so.

Forty cloves of garlic anyone?

In a friend's kitchen in a large house on the outskirts of the town, Floyd started to prepare a three-course lunch for all the people who had helped him when he ran his restaurant there. It was a lovely day and the children were playing outside in the orchard while the men drank pastis, that fiery aniseed spirit, on a small shady terrace at the back of the house. Floyd unpacked everything he'd bought in the market that morning: a kilo or so of little rockfish for the *soupe de poissons*, bunches of fat, moist garlic, a huge chicken with a long stretched neck and big yellow feet, and a couple of dozen apricots still attached to their stalks and leaves. It all made a very pretty picture lying on the scrubbed pine table.

Sometimes, annoyingly, when you are making television programmes, real life gets in the way of the process. Here we were, setting the scene for the beginning of our illuminating series on French food, but it was nearly midday and the people waiting outside in the garden were hungry. The French tend to get very agitated if lunch, their most important meal of the day, isn't ready by one. That meant Floyd would have to cook flat out and some form of compromise had to be made in terms of filming. We'd just have to busk it, without stopping to do any of the technical stuff that goes into the business of making television programmes, such as adjusting the lighting for the close-ups.

Today, in the background, away from the camera, there would probably be a couple of home economists chopping vegetables, making stock and generally doing all the donkey work necessary to start the various dishes. Next to the superstar chef the home economists are the mainstay of most current cooking programmes. They are the wise ones who have already tested the recipe and know the exact amounts of ingredients and cooking times. The days of the TV chef nipping out to the market and preparing the vegetables are long gone.

But in those naive days I had no idea such people existed. And even if I had known about them and could have afforded one, I don't think I would have taken a home economist on the shoot. Sometimes being overprepared can take away the fun – not that I've been overprepared for anything in my life. Instead, when the going got tough, or time was tight, it would be Andy or Timmy who would pick up a knife and help Keith out with the chopping.

Floyd rose admirably to the challenge and didn't hang around. He rubbed the chicken inside and out with salt and pepper, squeezed lemon juice all over and filled it up with cloves of purple garlic. He put it upside down into a medium hot oven and got on with the business of making the fish soup. All the time he was talking to the camera, telling the viewer exactly what he was doing, ever conscious of the fact that he hadn't got long to do it.

Clive slapped a new magazine onto the camera – bloody hell, that was the fourth one this morning – while Floyd was frying leeks, carrots and garlic in olive oil. He threw in some finely chopped celery and then in went a couple of sliced, fat, Provençal tomatoes, splashing a big splurge of hot oil on to the lens. Never mind. There was much hissing and spitting and clanking and scraping from the saucepan and from time to time the lens steamed up. Next he chucked in chopped fennel and onion. I sensed he was cooking in this brisk fashion because he knew it would be impossible to edit the film given the limitation of shots we would have in the time.

He gave a stir, poured water, about three or four pints, over the semi-fried vegetables, and now it was time, in true Floyd fashion, for a well-earned slurp of red wine before the water came to the boil: the moment to tip in that colourful assortment of little fish he had bought at the market earlier.

Towards the end of the cooking Keith called upon the lady of the house, Monique, to give him a hand. She was a stunning woman with hyacinth blue eyes and the blackest of black raven's-wing hair. She reminded me of a wilder version of Elizabeth Taylor and she would have been perfect playing Carmen. Rolling up her sleeves she started to put the cooked fish through a sieve, squeezing every large ladleful through the fine mesh so that all the goodness dripped through to the saucepan below. All the while Floyd spoke to her in a humorous and intimate way, which made her laugh and blush at the same time. I remember thinking, 'God! I wish I could speak French like that.' Such were the moments when I felt totally inadequate and quite envious of the talented Mr Floyd.

The meal of Provençal fish soup, followed by roast chicken cooked with forty cloves of garlic, and local apricots stuffed with goat's cheese, was a great success. The family and their friends sat around a long table under the dappled light filtering through the peach trees. It was like being in a poster advertising the joys of rural France: old and young sitting together laughing and enjoying the fruits of the land. It was a joy to film, while Floyd, after his mammoth cooking session against the clock, was lying back happily in a hammock in the cool of the orchard, a glass of wine in one hand and a cigarette in the other – the picture of contentment.

Contrary to what many people think, the crew rarely gets to try the food we've been filming all day. On this occasion it was gone three by the time we'd finished, and the boys were hungry. We said our goodbyes to the family and made our way to the nearest bar, the restaurants having closed over an hour before. The only thing left to eat were croques-monsieurs, toasted cheese sandwiches – Floyd and I preferred a cold beer and a cigarette – but everyone seemed very happy and excited, and it had been such a wonderfully productive first day. We were doing something completely new in the food repertoire of television. We had planned to film in six regions of France, Provence being the first, and, always the optimist, I could sense the start of a successful series.

As a director, even early on in a shoot, you can tell when things are working well. If they aren't, there are telltale signs. The first is the whistling. After a day's shoot everyone tends to give a hand to help pack the gear away, and if I hear a tuneless dirge as people pack the kit into the vehicles, trying to sound happy and carefree, I know to start to worry. Second comes a noticeable lack of eye contact, as if all of a sudden you've become invisible. Finally, and this is a real clincher, if the crew have got no time to have a parting drink, and all they want to know is the next day's call time, then you're in trouble.

Today, though, there were no such signs. We were all on a high. After a few drinks, the boys, being sensible, went back to the hotel to have a rest and put the camera gear out of harm's way while Keith, my assistant, Frances, and I continued to have a bit more to drink – quite a bit more, actually. By this time I was so happy I was thinking of turning the programmes into hour-long shows, although I'd only been commissioned to make a series of six half-hours.

Then, quite out of the blue, Keith brought me down to earth with a horrible bump. He had seemed to become a bit morose as late afternoon trickled into evening. Now I saw his eyes had turned into those hot coals I recognized from our first meeting at his bistro in Bristol.

'I want to be the producer of the programmes,' he announced. 'Or failing that the executive producer.'

I can't remember exactly what was said from that moment on, but it went something along these lines: 'Look, this whole show has been bankrolled by BBC Books and I write the book to accompany the series so therefore without me we wouldn't be here ...'

Well, I thought in my rather befuddled state, I suppose that's true, but equally without my recognizing your worth and taking a bit of a chance on *Floyd on Fish*, we wouldn't be sitting here, on a warm Provençal night, about to have an argument.

'Another thing that really gets to me,' he continued, 'is that you don't speak one bloody word of French and I've got to do all the translating. And you haven't a clue about the cooking of this country.'

Well, he had another point there, I suppose. I'd never seen fish soup made before. I didn't know that you could stuff apricots with goat's cheese. And previously I would have thought chicken roasted with forty or so cloves of garlic would be way too garlicky for the average person.

I thought of saying that it was true that I wasn't sophisticated when it came to food, but I did have an enormous love for the subject, not to mention a big appetite. And my inexperience could only help the process of making the programmes more accessible to the millions of people who wanted to learn about French regional cuisine, because sometimes television producers leave the audience behind by assuming they know the basic stuff when they don't. I felt that I instinctively knew how the programmes should look and feel, and I wanted to engage the viewers with that same sense of excitement that I felt when going to the market at L'Isle sur la Sorgue for the first time.

The Battle of Britain fighter pilots used to say, 'You can never spot Jerry when he comes from the sun.' By the time you find out, he's flown past leaving you with a cock-pit full of smoke and the stench of hot oil. Nothing works any more, the controls have gone limp and just as you think things couldn't be worse, the blighter's turning round and is about to give you another burst.

'I'm deeply unhappy with you, David, and I don't know how we're going to continue with this farce. It's pretty obvious you don't like the French – you keep going on about roast beef, pints of bitter, and fish and chips, not to mention the Hundred Years War – I just can't see us working like this for much longer and quite frankly I don't want to.'

I looked at Frances and she seemed close to tears. I thought Floyd and I had done so well in the relatively short time we'd been working together, and more impor-tantly I believed we'd become friends and despite our surface differences deep down had much in common. Clearly this was not the case. I'd been told stories of presenters turning into absolute monsters, but I naively thought that it took years to cultivate. This was quick by anyone's standards.

It was time to bail out. I gave him a burst from the eight Browning aircraft guns, before sliding back the canopy.

'Well, as for being the producer, you can fuck off! And if you don't want to carry on filming that's fine by me. All I can say is that it's a good job we found this out now. For what it's worth, I think you're a nasty little shit. I'll let the boys know in the morning and we'll drive back tomorrow.'

There were just a couple of rounds left and so I let fly for the final burst. 'And as for your book, you can stick it up your arse!'

There was so much more that I wanted to say, but with those parting words I went back, somewhat unsteadily, to the hotel.

Fortunately, Keith was staying with an old friend of his, Albert, who had a lovely house in the town. I think if we'd seen each other again later, we would have come to blows. For a while I sat at the small hotel bar drinking brandy and feeling very sorry for myself. Frances returned a half-hour or so later and she didn't say very much. She had only flown in from England that afternoon and she simply handed me a pile of mail, bound together with an elastic band. As if I was in any mood to read anything that night. Frances was very strict when it came to bad behaviour so I'm sure she disapproved of my awful language and I know she hadn't been impressed with Keith's performance either.

I woke up early the next morning because I'd forgotten to draw the curtains and the sun was streaming into this strange room, with its heavy tapestries, dark furniture and paintings of people in tall hats shooting ducks. I felt dreadful. I was seriously hung over and I'd just played over last night's scene with Keith in my mind. When things get this bad I usually gauge the problem with a simple test. Is it as bad, I ask myself, as Minnie Ripperton singing 'Lovin' You'? The answer, of course, is that nothing can be as bad as that.

Before the row with Keith, I'd planned to film a truffle hunter who lived near Mont Ventoux, a magical place dominating the landscape of the Rhône valley. But the wonderful landscape, the truffles, the wine, the sunflowers were now on hold. For the next miserable hour or so everything would have to be held in abeyance.

It was still early, so I wouldn't have to make any decisions just yet; not until it was time for breakfast. I sat on the lavatory reading the mail Frances had given me the night before. Suddenly I spotted a letter addressed in my own handwriting. Curious. I opened it and inside was a small slip of paper. Again, the handwriting was mine. All it said was, 'You are your own worst enemy.'

Then the penny dropped. About nine months previously I had been sent on a management course somewhere in the heart of Surrey. After three weeks of mucking about in the classroom, knowing deep in my heart that I'd never make a manager (I suspect everyone in the class did too), we were all asked to pen one sentence of insightful advice to ourselves. We were told that sometime in the future – perhaps in a few months, perhaps in a year – this would be sent to us and maybe, just maybe it would be useful. Who would have believed that such a prescient message would arrive at the very · moment it was most needed? I was so astonished I didn't quite know what to think, except that this message couldn't be ignored. I would seriously have to consider my future if I returned to the UK after filming for just one day because of some stupid, drunken disagreement. It would be a bit like going to see the headmaster because you'd been picked on in the school playground.

At breakfast Steve Williams, the lighting man, asked if he could have a quiet word. It seemed he knew all about the little fracas from the previous night. Apparently he had gone to the bar after I'd left to go back to the hotel, and he'd had a long chat with Keith, consoling him in his hour of need. Steve is a very gentle man, who speaks sound common sense. I think he would make a great psychiatrist. I told him about the odd letter I'd received from myself and he suggested the only way out of this mess was for Keith and me to meet like grown-ups and have a cup of coffee. And maybe I should try to be more complimentary about the French and not go on about the Hundred Years War being a jolly good thing. What a diplomat. I clearly had much to learn.

Well, Floyd and I did meet, and it was, to begin with, highly uncomfortable. He was having coffee with his friends from L'Isle sur la Sorgue, so I hung around and waited until they'd finished their conversation. Something he said to them obviously caused great amusement, and giving me a cursory nod, they left the bar one by one so I could join him. His eyes no longer had that piercing look. They were twinkling now, and he seemed in extremely good humour, which was more than could be said for me. It was true, he said, he did find it tiresome having to constantly cover for my virtually non-existent French, as well as turn in an acceptable piece to camera, and he did find my knowledge of French cuisine quite pathetic. However, he did see an advantage in that: if *I* could understand the subtle delights of French food then there was a fair chance that we might be able to success-fully present the whole gamut of French cuisine from Provence to Alsace to the viewers.

Another thing that annoyed him was that I kept call-ing him a 'restauranteur'. 'I'm not a fucking restauranteur, you pathetic secondary modern oik. I'm a restaurateur,' he would say on more than one occasion.

'Well, as a place where you eat is called a restaurant and not a 'restaurat',' I said now, holding my ground and strain-ing every syllable, 'it begs the question why the owner of such an establishment isn't called a 'restauranteur'.'

Restaurateur sounded to me like the equivalent of the Americans insisting on saying 'erbs' or the English trav-eller telling you he's just come back from *Barthelona*. However, I never called him a restauranteur again. I called him many other things, but not that.

This was a pivotal moment for us and although I didn't really want to, I apologized for my aggressive behaviour from the night before and wondered where we might go from here. Keith couldn't have been more friendly and amenable, and pretty soon we were in our cars, heading north-east for Mont Ventoux in search of the truffle hunter. There was no more talk about being the producer or executive producer.

Although the filming schedule was back on track I knew that the events of the previous night had changed everything for ever. Keith's relative fame had made him a much more brittle person to work with. This happens a great deal in television as presenters become more powerful and involved in the day to day business of making TV programmes, and it is why these days the title of executive producer is often given away to difficult presenters like a free jar of toffees. But at that moment I was unprepared for this sudden shift of balance. It felt a bit like working with the ugly duckling and getting to like him, only to discover that suddenly he's turned into an enormous great swan without you noticing.

The pelican

A few weeks later we found ourselves near the Lascaux caves, where the earliest paintings known to man were found. These go back nearly twenty thousand years and they beautifully depict bulls, bison, and horses in motion. On a nearby river we filmed a memorable scene with the aforementioned fisherman, Monsieur Le Pélican, so called because he had an extremely large nose. I thought of Cyrano de Bergerac as we were shaking hands. In fact, the town of Bergerac was just a few miles distant so maybe, I thought, large hooters were a feature of the region.

It was early, the sun had only just come over the horizon and the mist was still swirling on the calm surface of the river as the Pelican and Floyd made their way to the centre in an old wooden punt, while we filmed them through a telephoto lens from the riverbank. Although he appeared to be in his mid-sixties the Pelican was extremely muscular and formidably strong, and as we filmed he stood on the bow and threw a net about twenty yards in a perfect arc. The small metal weights at the bottom of the net flashed in the sunlight and it grew larger, opening up like a flower as it flew through the air. By the time it splashed on to the surface it had formed a perfect silver circle about ten feet in diameter.

The Pelican waited until the net had touched the bottom of the river and then slowly started to pull it in. It was a timeless, extraordinarily powerful scene that wouldn't have seemed out of place depicted on the ancient walls of the Lascaux caves.

Back on land the Pelican showed us his catch. It wasn't great, but he had a few nice perch, which are freshwater bass really. They are extremely handsome fish with olive green stripes and red fins and I've always been fond of them because I'd caught lots of them as a boy. He had quite a few gudgeon too. Once the mainstay of a poor family's country diet, they are tiny fish about the size of a thumb and good to eat. There were dace, silver bream, roach, and rudd as well – the sort of fish we'd never dream of eating back at home these days.

Using my camping stove, Floyd created a nice little lunch with them for the Pelican. After scaling and gutting an assortment, but mostly the gudgeon, he dusted them in seasoned flour and fried them in goose fat (this being the Périgord) until they were golden, then tossed some chopped flat leaf parsley and new season's garlic over the top.

The Pelican seemed impressed and they washed the meal down with a bottle of local red that had been cooling in the river. I didn't know at the time, but weeks later, while editing the film, I discovered the Pelican had quoted that old proverb, 'Give a man a fish and he lives for a day. Teach a man to fish and he lives for a lifetime.' Someone told me that American anglers in Florida have adapted that to 'Give a man a fish and he lives for a day. Teach a man to fish and he'll drink beer all day.'

I do believe in ghosts and I'd like to imagine that in centuries to come, if you went to that part of the Dordogne in the early morning, at the moment the sun rises in high summer, when the white mists dance and swirl over the mirrored surface of the river, before the hot sun kills them off ... if you looked hard enough, you might make out the shape of a tall man with a very large nose, perfectly casting a silver net.

The old battleaxe

Madame Moulin was a farmer's wife who looked like a strict headmistress straight from Central Casting, right down to her steel-rimmed spectacles and sensible shoes. She was in her mid-fifties, lean and strong and she was watching in disbelief as we filmed Floyd cooking a mushroom omelette in her kitchen. He wasn't using normal common or garden mushrooms, the kind that we know and love at home. These were the highly revered ceps, very handsome members of the fungi family that look like button mushrooms on steroids. The Italians are also passionate about them and call them *porcini*, 'baby pigs'.

Madame Moulin and her husband had a small farm and to make ends meet they took in paying guests. Agriculture tourism is a great success now in Europe, especially in France and Italy, but it was relatively new in the mid-Eighties. I suspected the idea was actually a British invention from the Fifties, except that we called it 'farming holidays' which probably didn't sound bureaucratic enough for Brussels.

The evening before we filmed with Madame, Floyd, me, and the whole crew had had a typical Périgordian supper at her modest farmhouse. The food relied entirely, apart from a memorable prune tart, on duck, the gastronomic icon of this region. We started with a duck terrine made with wild morel mushrooms and Armagnac. Then a large bowl of duck gizzards cooked in red wine appeared in the middle of the table. I noticed some nervous glances among the crew as Madame Moulin ladled huge amounts into the biggest white soup plates I'd ever set eyes on. I hadn't a clue what a gizzard was. I'd only ever heard the word spoken in pirate films, normally after a ship had been captured and someone like Robert Newton would draw his cutlass and say. 'Aaaaargh! [menacing eyeballs staring straight at camera] Let's slit their throats, lads, and feed their gizzards to the sharks!'

Now we were about to eat them and they looked as if they were being served in bowls of blood. None of us were in a hurry to start, so when Madame popped out to the kitchen I looked to Keith for some kind of reassurance.

'They're the bits like little food processors inside the birds' stomachs that grind up everything they eat,' he said, cutting one up.

I've had gizzards quite often since, and sliced thinly, fried in duck fat, then tossed through a salad they are quite superb. These, though, were as tough as old boots, despite their good flavour.

Madame Moulin reappeared, asking if everything was all right.

'*Oui*,' we chanted in unison, '*formidable*.'

Once she had disappeared again Keith mustered all his remaining gizzards onto a side plate, tipped the lot into a handkerchief and put it in the pocket of his blazer. He sat there beaming triumphantly while we soldiered on. Most of us had at least half a dozen of the wretched muscular things to get through. Now I do think it's important to eat everything that's put in front of you on these occasions. We were ambassadors for our country and we were going to be filming there the next day. But you can't hurry gizzards, no matter how you try. When Madame returned again she was most upset that Monsieur Floyd was the only one sitting there with an empty plate. Keith patted his stomach as though he was full and said the gizzards were absolutely delicious. Tutting and clucking her tongue like a mother hen she filled his bowl up again. Keith looked around at us for support and asked – though it sounded more like pleading – if anyone would care for some more gizzards? No takers. Laurence Olivier couldn't have done a better job of portraying an English gourmet enjoying every morsel of those gizzards as Madame Moulin stood there with the pride of a mother watching a baby taking its first solid food.

Fortunately she didn't understand me admonishing Keith in my best Monty Python voice. 'Now, you naughty boy, I want to see all those gizzards gone. Otherwise you're having gizzards for breakfast and gizzards for lunch, and if you don't eat them all, you'll have gizzards for tea!'

The next morning we filmed in Madame Moulin's kitchen. The original plan had been for Keith to prepare a cep omelette for her and her husband to taste afterwards. I was hoping that they would share their honest thoughts with him and maybe add a few tips. However, when Madame turned out to be such a bossy character I thought it would be a much funnier idea if she could stand behind Keith like a buzzard, watching his every move. And what a good idea it was too. She didn't like one single thing he did, from the way he moved the raw egg around the pan to the timing of dropping the sliced ceps into the half-cooked egg, or the seasoning. Everything he attempted was considered a travesty by Madame Moulin. I honestly think it would be impossible to shoot a sequence like that today, because most television chefs' egos are so large they would find it too belittling, and they and their agents simply wouldn't allow it to be broadcast. But when the programme was shown on TV, it was this sequence that, more than any other, endeared the British public to the beleaguered Floyd. In the end Keith confessed to the camera how painful it was cooking in front of this old battleaxe.

'How would she like it if she was cooking roast lamb, new potatoes and runner beans on an unfamiliar stove in Somerset, while his mother breathed down her neck?'

Finally she declared his efforts inedible because the omelette was far too soft for her liking and the ceps weren't cooked enough.

'OK,' he said, 'if you're so blimmin' clever lady – you cook it!'

And with that she set about the serious business of making a cep omelette Périgordian farmer's-wife style, which, to our surprise, turned out to be rather like a Spanish tortilla, quite hard and pliable. Apparently this was because it was designed to be taken out into the fields for the workers to eat, so it mustn't fall apart. By contrast Floyd's omelette was beautifully soft and fluffy and designed to withstand the short walk from kitchen to restaurant table.

'Well', he said, '*vive la différence!*'

Through a glass darkly

We stopped for a few days in Gevrey Chambertin. Napoleon enjoyed the wines from the nearby château of Chambertin so much he ordered his troops to salute the vineyards as they marched past on their way to various campaigns. The French infantry do so to this day. My trusty film crew and I adopt this same token of appreciation when we salute the butcher's shop in the village of Tideford for their excellent joints of beef and fine pasties, on our way down to Padstow to film with Rick Stein.

In Gevrey we stayed in a hotel on a vineyard run by an exceptionally beautiful blonde woman who wore shiny black leather dresses and the reddest lipstick and nail varnish I'd ever seen. Madame Le Clerc was her name, and maybe my life in Plymouth had been too sheltered, but I found it very difficult to take my eyes off her. Although she was of a 'certain age', she was like a cross between the singer Blondie and a starlet from *The Brides of Dracula*. As if in character, she produced huge blood red glasses of Kir Cardinal, made from Madame's pinot noir and double strength crème de cassis, which tasted like an alcoholic blackcurrant cordial.

It was pretty clear to all that Madame only had eyes, and ears, for Keith, who had arrived immaculately dressed, naturally, in a blazer, sporting a blue and white spotted cravat, like Tony Curtis imitating Cary Grant in *Some Like It Hot*. They were deep in animated conversation, however something was clearly annoying her because in-between pouring cassis into the enormous balloon-shaped crystal glasses, she kept saying '*merde*' and hitting the top of the bar with a clenched fist.

'She's fed up because tomorrow is the start of the harvest, the *vendange*, and it's up to her to feed about thirty hungry grape pickers breakfast, lunch, and dinner, but the most important of these is lunch,' Floyd explained.

'What is she going to cook for them?' I asked.

Madame Le Clerc threw me a baleful glare; well, at least she acknowledged I was there. They conversed for a few more seconds and then she threw out her hands and blew air from her fulsome red lips: pofffff! – the way the French do when they think that something is ridiculous.

'Why don't you come to her rescue by cooking lunch?' I said.

To my amazement, he thought it was a terrific idea, a real challenge. He asked Madame Le Clerc for a piece of paper and began to write his menu.

'First course,' he announced with a flourish, 'will be crudités. Grated celeriac with mayonnaise and salads of tuna, tomato and fresh basil, tossed in really good olive oil.' He was in his element now, his pencil racing over the page as fast as he could write, like Gershwin penning 'Rhapsody in Blue'. 'Then mounds of hot scarlet radishes dipped in unsalted butter, rich pork farmhouse terrines, fat white asparagus and slices of Bayonne ham with Dijon mustard.' Madame was nearly fainting with admiration. 'Then, for the main course, coq au vin, the classic dish from this part of the world, made with old birds that have done their fair share of pecking round the farmyard.'

I gave Madame a cursory glance to see if she had read a little innuendo in that last description, but fortunately she hadn't.

He continued writing his shopping list and then Madame whispered something to him.

He looked at me and said with a serious face, 'The food has to be top notch because the pickers are serious connoisseurs and very fussy, and if it's not right, they'll walk out, leaving the grapes on the vine.'

And so the stage was set for the following day.

How wonderful it was to be out with the grape pickers, mostly local students from the nearby city of Dijon, when the air was still cold and you could see their frosty breath rising above the vines, heavy with dusty purple bunches of pinot noir. We filmed the pickers singing as they snipped the bunches and put them gently into the large wicker baskets they carried on their backs in the way their mothers and fathers, grandmothers and grandfathers had done before them. Back at the hotel Floyd seem to be disappearing behind a mound of jointed chicken. Andy MacCormack and our new interpreter, Debbie Donlin, were helping him and there was a certain tension in the air. The happy mood of the previous evening had evaporated and been replaced by grim determination.

'Another fine mess you've got me into, Pritchard,' was my greeting. 'How do you expect me to cook coq au vin for thirty ravenous grape pickers when I've only got a poxy domestic cooker to work on. And what's more it's electric.'

Just as I had thought everything was going so well. Not only was the cooker not up to the job, but every time we turned on our lights for filming it stopped working altogether. Meanwhile the clock was ticking. It occurred to me that it might have been an idea to have dragged ourselves away from Madame's Kir Cardinals the night before, and checked out her kitchen before we committed Floyd to cooking lunch. Because it was a hotel it was bound to have a heavy-duty cooker, I had thought, but now I reminded myself that the animal with the long trunk and a penchant for buns is not necessarily an elephant. Never assume, David, always check.

Floyd had poured several bottles of Gevrey Chambertin into a couple of enormous saucepans. It made me want to cry just thinking about it, but Madame insisted we must use her wine for the dish. He dropped in fresh thyme, bay leaves, an onion stuck with cloves, a couple of sticks of celery and carrots, and about half a dozen cloves of garlic, bashed and bruised, with their skins still on. The volume of wine had to evaporate by half and then it had to be strained of all those ingredients to form the all important base for this classic Sixties bistro dish. Fortunately we had managed to film this stage, but now we would have to continue without lights. Floyd and Andy sautéed the chicken pieces until they were golden and then worked flat out frying pieces of pancetta, little onions and mushrooms, ready to add the lot to the reduced sauce.

It was approaching eleven o'clock, and even though the filming lights were switched off, the cooker kept conking out. Finally there was a loud bang, followed by a smell of burning and then *nothing* worked. The hotel was now completely without electricity and the meal for the grape pickers was beginning to look decidedly precarious. Madame swept into the kitchen with a very worried-looking husband in tow. Today her hair was tied in a bun and she was wearing a bright, figure-hugging red dress. She gave me a withering look, then picked up one of the heavy saucepans, instructed Floyd to do the same and led the way, weaving through cars, across the busy N74 outside the vineyard. On the other side,

Monsieur Le Clerc banged on his neighbours' doors, hoping they weren't in the middle of cooking their own lunch. Even if they had been, I suspect the people round there would have summed up the urgency of the situation in an instant. It wasn't long before the two large pots were gently simmering on the stoves of two adjoining neighbours' cottages. It looked like we would make it after all.

A few minutes after twelve, two tractors, their trailers full of hungry pickers, arrived in the courtyard of the hotel. A long table that ran the length of an outbuilding was laid with the crudités, salads, bread, cheeses, ham, terrines and wine, and the pickers wasted no time in sitting down and helping themselves. The young people were ravenous and they ate and drank with noisy abandon. It could have been a scene from a Breughel painting except these harvesters wore baseball caps and Nike T-shirts. When it was time to bring on the heavy pots of coq au vin the *vendangeurs* cheered and clapped and Madame and Floyd filled up plates and passed them down the table. Bowls of steaming boiled potatoes appeared from nowhere to accompany the chicken. Despite the morning's dramas the lunch was a huge success and Madame even flashed me a smile. When the pickers had finished eating they insisted on singing to honour the chef who had put so much effort into creating lunch for so many people, in the space of a few hours. As they were climbing back onto the trailers to go back to work, I asked what they had really thought of the meal. Unanimously they said it was the best they'd eaten in all the time they had been picking grapes. Sometimes, they told me, the food was poor, perhaps just some soup and bread, maybe a terrine, and some rough wine – not good enough to make them relish the thought of coming back the next day. At other times the lunches were pretty good, but this one had been exceptional. And would the chef be back tomorrow?

When the balloon goes up

From my hotel room, through the early evening mist I could see the rooftops of a small town in Alsace where storks were building their huge nests in chimney pots and on top of telegraph poles. The surrounding fields were full of cabbages the size of basketballs that seemed to be rotting in the ground. Apparently that's how the locals like them for making sauerkraut. They do the same with their grapes too, leaving them on the vine so that the first frosts of autumn cause them to shrivel and wrinkle. To the untrained eye it looks as if disaster has struck, but here they call it 'noble rot', from which they make their famous sweet wine to be drunk with desserts and cheese.

I really liked Alsace, partly because the food was hearty and the portions generous. A typical meal might start off with liver dumplings, followed by sausages and boiled ham with lashings of hot sauerkraut. But the main reason I liked it was the lovely pubs. In most parts of France, from Provence to Normandy, the bars would usually be full of pressed steel, chrome, and plastic furniture, dominated by huge television sets pumping out old series of

Falcon Crest, with youths playing non-stop table football. But in Alsace, from what I had seen of it, the bars were more like English pubs and people came to them because the beer was so good.

It was in one of these pubs in the town of Colmar that I met up with the great-grandson of Albert Schweitzer, the Nobel prize-winning missionary doctor, the male equivalent of Mother Theresa, who built Lambaréné hospital in Africa nearly a hundred years ago. His name was Andre Graf and he wore a bright red flying suit which made him look every inch like the famous Red Baron. He'd heard that we had been filming around Colmar and suggested that it would be a great idea to shoot a sequence in his hot air balloon. What a stroke of luck, I thought. I could see the scene: Floyd, glass of wine in hand, looking down from the wicker basket as the light turned to gold over all those lovely vineyards and farms and forests hundreds of feet below.

Surrounded by his ballooning friends, who reminded me of that old slapstick trio the Three Stooges, Andre dunked his finger into his glass of beer and started to draw the route for the balloon on the bar.

'We take off here, in the foothills of the Vosges Mountains', (represented by a packet of cashews), 'and we drift gently down this valley.' I watched his finger leave a trail of Pils Lager, 'which will take us to the Rhine [a packet of Gauloise]. Then,' he said, expansively, 'we will land and we shall have an early lunch with much Crémant d'Alsace' – this was the local sparkling blend of pinot noir and chardonnay. 'Don't worry,' he said 'the balloon is much safe.'

Well, I thought, what could be easier? And what a valuable visual contribution this would be to our programme.

At that point we were joined in the bar by a rather grumpy Keith, who had had a bit of a headache that afternoon and had gone back to the hotel to sleep it off. I introduced him to Andre and his ballooning friends and began to tell Keith the plan. He didn't look terribly pleased and seemed quite concerned about the safety of such an endeavour.

'Don't worry, I am a serious balloon pilot with many hours of flying experience. There is nothing that can go wrong,' said Andre.

'How do you know this man is competent enough to fly a balloon?' Floyd wanted to know. 'You've only just met him.'

'Look, it's a bit rude to talk this way in front of Andre,' I told him, 'and anyway he's Albert Schweitzer's great-grandson, and he's got a badge of a balloon on his flying suit, so he must know what he's doing.'

Sensing a degree of tension, Andre stood up and said he would come to get us at five the next morning. Floyd glared at me for the rest of the evening.

The next morning, through beeswing eyes, the weather looked glorious and the mist was clearing in the valleys that led to the heavily wooded slopes of the Vosges Mountains. Suddenly, as Andre steered his four-wheel drive up the tortuous roads to the launch site, I realized where I heard the name of this mountain range before. It was here, many years ago, that a millionaire playboy was killed in a light plane. I remembered reading the story of how he was desperate to see his lover, an actress who lived in the south of France, and he forced his pilots to fly over this mountain range in a terrible storm. They were found days later with handkerchiefs stuffed in their mouths to stop them biting off their tongues when they crash landed. I couldn't get those images out of my head. Bloody hell, I thought, at least they weren't in a balloon. Nevertheless, I thought it best not to share the story with Keith.

By the time we arrived at the launch site, the big red balloon was half inflated.

Keith puffed on his cigarette, looking ruffled. 'How, I ask you, are we going to fit into *that*?' he said, pointing to the wicker basket.

It was only about four foot square, which meant that Floyd and Clive would have to go with Andre, while the rest of us would have to stay behind. I tried to put on a really sad face, one that said, 'I have been waiting all my life for a moment like this but now it has been snatched away from me at the last minute.' Except I couldn't stop myself from smiling.

One by one the ropes that tethered the balloon to the ground were untied. I made sure that Keith had a glass of wine to sip while describing his gentle flight down the valleys to the banks of the Rhine. When they started to rise into the misty air we suddenly realized that Frances was still holding on to one of the ropes. Everyone shouted in unison for her to let go and she dropped to the ground from about four or five feet in the air. Without Frances hanging on, the balloon picked up speed and started to soar above us.

I well remember Keith's parting words just before they flew out of earshot. 'I hope you fucking well know what you're doing, Pritchard!'

These were the days when the words health and safety hadn't become stuck together like husband and wife, and Keith, as I've said, was a brave man.

The crew and I were in a perfect position to see the balloon float gently down the valley, but it seemed to be rising higher and higher in the sky as if it was about to fly in the opposite direction over the dreaded Vosges Mountains. No, it must be an optical illusion, I thought, but the expressions on the faces of Andre's colleagues told a different story. Suddenly, excited chatter came over their walkie-talkie.

Of course, I couldn't understand a word but from the way they jumped into their jeep and roared off up the mountain track, his message could well have been, 'Which of you two idiots checked the weather forecast this morning? Because we're being blown across the Vosges Mountains, and not down the fucking valley … so help!'

In a nutshell, the wind was blowing the wrong way. I tried to blank out the image of those poor pilots with their handkerchiefs in their mouths, and suggested we all pile into the cars and follow the balloon.

I learnt a lot about balloons that day. First, in order to float gently down a valley you need a certain amount of gas to keep the balloon aloft. Second, and more importantly, to climb to a great height in order to clear mountain tops you need to have much more gas; unbeknown to me at the time, that was what Andre didn't have.

On one side of the mountain road we were driving up was a wall of solid rock, and on the other, where the sky should be, was a curtain of pine trees, some of the tallest I'd ever seen, through which I was frantically trying to catch a glimpse of the giant flying plum tomato. In a break in the trees we came to a lay-by, one of those spots for tourists to take photographs because the view is so spectacular, but in all of the great big blue sky there was no sign of the balloon. The curious thing was I still believed that Andre knew what he was doing and would keep Keith and Clive safe; and, though I feel ashamed to admit it, I was also thinking, 'If they do have to crash-land I hope Clive will keep the camera running.' It would make a great sequence.

We carried on driving and then, coming down the hill towards me, I saw a familiar four-wheel-drive vehicle. It was pulling a trailer and on it was a wicker basket. In the fleeting seconds as they passed me, I could see Keith and Clive inside with Andre. They were alive. I had to drive for miles before I could find a place to turn around, so it was a good ten minutes later that I found them in a field way down in the valley. Since there was not enough gas for them to clear the mountains, they had had to make a very scary emergency landing onto the main road, squeezing through that narrow gap between the mountainside and the tops of the pines. To make it through, they had to come down fast. Apparently what happens is that a flap is released at the top of the balloon and, as the warm air rushes out, the basket and its occupants hurtle to earth like a stone.

Floyd's eyes had turned into those familiar hot coals as I approached him to say how relieved and happy I was to find them both alive and well. If looks could kill, I wouldn't be sitting here now at my kitchen table, writing this.

It's probably best if I try to forget the rest of the exchange, peppered as it was with expletives, while beside us, Andre, feeling that perhaps we all needed cheering up, used the remaining gas on-board the balloon to cool a bottle of the promised Crémant d'Alsace. That was the last straw for Keith.

'I can't believe I'm seeing this. Here's this idiot who said he didn't have enough gas on-board to fly safely over the mountains, and now here he is using it to chill a bottle of wine. I think you're all barking mad, and as for you Pritchard, it'll be days – possibly weeks – before I speak to you again.'

And with that he asked Frances to drive him back to the hotel in Colmar immediately.

I wondered if Clive had managed to film the crash-landing. He said that actually he had been quite busy using his body to protect the camera as the descent, though very skilfully done, involved virtually a straight drop from thirty feet. Not only was that just a bit terrifying, but the basket, on touchdown, had tipped over, spilling the three of them onto the road.

'Oh well, never mind,' I nearly said. But didn't.

Please sir, the dog ate my homework

When the editing was complete it was time to go to the dubbing theatre. This is the equivalent of putting the icing on the cake and it very often marked the end of a long and sometimes difficult journey. Dubbing theatres are expensive places to work in because the sophisticated equipment and the highly skilled dubbing mixers don't come cheap. So it is vital that all the necessary preparatory work, like the writing of scripts, is done beforehand. This is a golden rule and one that should be treated with the utmost respect.

Writing commentaries is a pretty tiresome affair because you have to run the pictures time and again to ensure the words complement them. There were always scenes that needed illuminating in Keith's dulcet tones, shots of him driving through the countryside, dare I say it, ballooning, and any amount of footage aboard fishing boats. A commentary is an exact art and although the finished result should sound relaxed it takes time and patience to do well. Usually, I would allow a day with Floyd to write a thirty-minute commentary. We would start off by looking at the film and airing our thoughts aloud then we'd start to scribble things down on paper until we had something we thought would work.

The first couple of hours normally went well and then as the clock ticked its way towards midday Keith would say, 'I think this would work a lot better if we stopped for a little heart starter and then a spot of lunch.'

And who was I to disagree?

A 'heart starter' meant at least a couple of pints of bitter for me and two, or three, large whiskies for Keith, followed by lunch at the Italian restaurant, the Hosteria de Romana on Plymouth's Barbican. After a couple of outings there Floyd christened it the Hysteria Romana. We'd normally start with large bowls of spaghetti with clams cooked with plenty of garlic and chopped parsley, accompanied by Chianti. Then we'd move on to perfectly cooked saltimbocca, washed down with even more Chianti. Saltimbocca – a veal escalope with Parma ham and lots of fresh sage, roasted in the oven with olive oil – literally means 'jump in the mouth'. This would be followed by amarettis and coffee. The food was good and it heightened our spirits as we talked passionately about the film we'd been scrutinizing most of the morning. Such lunch stops, we felt, brought out brilliant ideas, which was just as well as they also meant that we would often break the cardinal rule and turn up at the dubbing theatre, at the BBC in Bristol, without a finished script.

The theatre was run by a fiery Scot called Stuart Grieg who, fortunately for us, entered into the humorous spirit of our 'creative lunches'.

Floyd would look at shots of the mighty River Rhône on the large screen, then say something like 'The River Rhône is very long and very wide and the French like it very much indeed. I like it too because it cuts a swathe through the greatest gastronomic heartland of the world on its long journey to the Mediterranean Sea.'

When he came to an end we'd all clap and whistle and ask him to say a bit more – maybe another ten seconds – to finish it off.

He'd clear his throat, take a sip from a weak whisky and water and continue with gusto. 'This river, this wonderful river [this would be with a slight Churchillian flourish] blesses all it touches along its banks with almonds, cherries, peaches, and plums. Here is the land that gave us the cassoulet and rich Gigondas wine. More than that, a hundred years ago, it opened the eyes of one jaded Dutch artist to the splendours of the sun and instead of potatoes he painted sunflowers.'

'Hurray!' we'd all shout out and then we'd play it back to see if it fitted the pictures. This was great fun and very often Stuart would dart out of the dubbing suite and return a few minutes later clutching a disc. He'd put it on the record player and the chosen music, combined with Floyd's commentary, would turn a selection of beautiful pictures of a slow moving river into something quite moving and heartfelt.

One must never underestimate the power of sound. On one occasion we were in the studio watching scenes we had shot of Keith cooking a stew on Hadrian's Wall in Northumberland on a cold March day. The night before filming we'd met a man in a pub who was very interested in the Romans and how they lived during the time they occupied Britain. I thought it would be a great idea, using this man's expert guidance, for Keith to create the sort of dish that the legionnaires might have prepared 2,000 years before. So he made a beef stew with parsnips, flavoured with honey and liquamen sauce. This famous condiment was made from fermented anchovies – a bit like our Worcestershire sauce – and it was carried by most Roman soldiers. They probably thought the food of the

169

native Britons quite atrocious and wanted to spice it up with something from home. A bit like Brits taking bottles of tomato ketchup and HP sauce on holiday to Spain.

In a cast iron pot simmering over an open fire Keith did his best to produce a dish that might have been eaten by the sentries guarding the nearby fortress of Vindolanda. He had brought along his ingredients in enamelled tins, and as he was cooking, he'd throw the empty ones aside. Stuart, the wily dubbing mixer, created a sound that made them smash like crystal glass. Not content with that he also imitated the sound of a dog yelping with pain as though it had just been hit. When he ran all the soundtracks together the result was quite bizarre and very funny. There was Keith doing his level best to cook in these inclement conditions, while every time he tossed a dish aside there was a loud smash, accompanied by a canine howl. The BBC, I'm told, received many complaints about cruelty to the poor little stray dog the viewers imagined had found refuge near the fire where Keith was cooking. One lady even seemed convinced that it was a brown and white spaniel.

On one of my many trips to the dubbing theatre in Bristol from my home on the outskirts of Plymouth I picked up a hitchhiker on the A38 on a cold, brooding March day. I had a rather battered and rusty Peugeot 504 at the time. After a few miles the chap inevitably asked what I did for a living and I told him that I made the Keith Floyd programmes for the BBC. There was a strained silence and he spent most of the next hour pointedly looking out of his passenger window. Clearly he thought I was some weirdo, because a real TV producer wouldn't be driving around in a rusty old Peugeot. I was just making a vow to myself never to give a hitchhiker a lift again, when there was a loud blast of a car horn and a large white Bentley pulled alongside. Sitting in the front passenger seat was Floyd, indicating to me to wind down my window. This was a huge mistake, as after a couple of turns of the winder, the whole pane of glass dropped into the door frame with a resounding thump, like a blade from a guillotine. In my moment of surprise I'd forgotten that the window had only two positions: open and closed. Keith shouted something about seeing me in the dubbing theatre and gave the universal drinker's sign of raising an invisible glass to the lips and waggling his fingers. I assume his chauffeur saw that as the signal that this brief meeting on the motorway had come to an end, because he shot off up the M5 like a bat out of hell and disappeared into the distance. I was left behind, with a freezing cold wind whistling through the car, as I kept my old 504 plodding along at sixty, in case the engine overheated.

My hitchhiker suddenly became quite animated. 'So you *really* know Keith Floyd,' he said. 'Sorry, what was it that you said you do? I was thinking of going into television myself, actually, and they say it's not what you know it's *who* you know.'

I must have heard this a hundred times, so I turned the radio up and looked forward with longing to the moment when I would see Brunel's masterpiece of a suspension bridge spanning the River Avon at Clifton.

PART VII

A slice of American pie

'Recce' trips are a bit like holidays with a purpose, a culinary journey of six weeks or so touring fishing ports, restaurants, markets, breweries, cheese-makers and distillers, looking for places to film. It's a lovely job.

It was 1988 and I had decided to make my way across America, from California to Florida, to research locations for Floyd's *American Pie*, a series we'd planned to shoot in a few months' time. After finding some great cooks in San Francisco, where I savoured clam chowder from a Styrofoam cup on Fisherman's Wharf, I decided on a whim to go to Dallas, because I loved the TV series, but after a couple of non-eventful days there I hired a car and from the map I found in the glovebox, I pinpointed the town of Paris around five hours' drive away. I'd heard of the famous low budget horror film *The Cars that Ate Paris* and thought it would an exciting place to visit. I didn't know at the time that the Paris in the film was, in fact, a small town in Australia, which might have accounted for the blank and confused expressions on the faces of the locals, when I explained my reason for coming to this small Texan town.

It took me most of the day to get there and I was gasping for a beer. The town centre was made up of Thirties

175

shops and commercial buildings, the sort of town in which you might find James Stewart playing a salt-of-the-earth local lawyer. When he wasn't pacing up and down in the courthouse confusing the prosecution witnesses with his homespun rhetoric, he'd put up a sign on his office door that said 'Gone Fishing'. It was that sort of place. Everything seemed to be closed, including, to my horror, the bars.

It was starting to get dark and I heard a distant roll of thunder and felt a few drops of rain. A passing local explained that as it was a Sunday, alcohol was forbidden, and the only place to find a drink was at the Holiday Inn on the outskirts of town. I needed a place to stay the night, so, through raindrops the size of 50p pieces that were exploding on my windscreen, I searched the skyline for the familiar green neon sign.

They say that everything in Texas is bigger and brasher than anywhere else in the country and that was certainly true of the thunderstorm that was erupting all around me. Super-bright lightning was followed relentlessly by massive crashes of thunder. Bernard Herrmann's soundtrack from Hitchcock's *Psycho* kept playing eerily in my mind, in time to the swish, swish, swishing of the windscreen wipers, as I spotted the sign for the motel. There was no one on the desk. I rang the bell and shouted, but no one came. Still, there was music and laughter coming from a room opposite the reception area which, joy of joys, turned out to be the bar. The flashes of lightning cut through the gloom, silhouetting a bunch of men wearing cowboy hats. I ordered a beer and asked if I could book a room. The barman said I was the only person staying that night and I should park my car in front of whichever cabin I liked. Tell him the number and he'd give me the key.

I ordered another beer, while I waited for the raging storm to subside, and a man with a red beard jutting out at an unusual angle from his chin came and sat beside me. He had guessed I was English and told me he was a distant cousin to the Queen.

'That's very nice,' I said. Did he see her very often?

He told me he hadn't actually been to England, but was planning a trip soon. I thought this would be a good moment to find my room, but it was still lashing down. So I ordered another beer.

The man with the red beard asked what I was doing in Paris, Texas. I told him I was researching a television programme about American food for the BBC.

'Go no further,' he said, coming right up close. 'You wanna taste the best chilli cornbread in the whole of Texas? Well, come with me to my farm. I've got my pickup right outside.'

'Well, thanks very much,' I said, trying to show genuine appreciation, 'but I've been driving all day and I'm very tired and I just want a beer. Besides it's pouring with rain.'

He was quiet for a minute and then he asked if I'd ever heard of the Holy Grail.

'Of course,' I said.

'Do you know where it is?' he countered.

'Um, somewhere in the south of France, buried under some ancient church on top of a mountain, I suspect.' I'd just read *The Holy Blood and the Holy Grail*, so I felt sure of my subject.

'No it ain't,' he replied angrily. 'It's sitting right on top of my TV set. *Now* will you come back and try my chilli cornbread?'

Nervously, I feigned tiredness and told him that under normal circumstances I'd *love* to come and see his Grail but I was dead beat.

'I'll let you drink wine from the Grail,' he persisted, 'and you'll feel the power of our Lord surge through your arms until your whole body feels like it's going to explode. Don't you want to feel that power?'

'Er, no thank you. I'm going to bed now.' And I ran away.

'Come rain, come lightning, come thunder, you have become my friends and I love you,' I thought as I made my way to the car. Any amount of lashing rain was preferable to Redbeard. I wanted to lock myself in a room, draw the curtains and barricade the door, but first I had to choose my cabin and return to that God-awful bar for my key.

I chose a cabin right in the middle of a line of around thirty, then made my way under a sheltered wooden boardwalk back to the bar. Redbeard was still there, talking to a couple of his mates, so I avoided the temptation to have another beer and retreated to the cabin with my key. The lightning had short-circuited the electricity supply, so with the flashes lighting up the room every few seconds, and the soundtrack to the *Psycho* shower-sequence stabbing away in my ears, I chained the door and piled as much furniture as I could shift in front of it. To make matters worse I was ravenous. All I'd eaten all day was some fried chicken with turnip greens and grits at a roadside stop not far from Dallas. Grits, for the uninitiated, are boiled grains of corn cooked to the consistency of a thin porridge: America's answer to polenta. I think you must have to go on a special course to understand and appreciate grits. The hotel's restaurant was closed so I raided the mini bar for Beer Nuts, which I ate in the darkness. Then I phoned Floyd and told him where I was, boarded up in a motel in Texas, and that should anything happen to me, it was the strange bloke with the mad eyes and the jutting red beard who had done it. He thought it was terribly funny, but I was being deadly serious.

I'd seen the scene so many times before at the cinema. You know the one; the hero hears the footsteps of the bad guy coming down the boardwalk and then you see the door handle of the cabin start to turn, and you hear the click, click, click. Now I was right there in the movie. On the drive here I had imagined myself arriving in Paris and tucking into a thick, juicy sixteen-ounce entrecôte steak with sweet golden fat, accompanied by an extremely large glass of Napa's finest red. The restaurant would probably look like the Cattleman's Club in the *Dallas* TV series, with happy families tucking into ribs and sirloins all around me, laughing and joshing with each other. I thought of the things I would order as 'sides' – baked potatoes with soured cream perhaps, or French fries and a green salad. Instead, here I was cowering in the dark, drinking bourbon from a miniature bottle, eating a miserable bag of nuts, and waiting for some nutcase to break into my room. No doubt carrying a shotgun.

When I woke up the next morning, everything was clear and bright. My car was the only one in a car park full of puddles the size of duck ponds. I had missed breakfast so I drove back to town, to an old-fashioned family-style restaurant I had spotted the previous day on my desperate hunt for a bar. It was a busy place with a big shop window, and from the pavement you could see the customers tucking into their meals. I guessed the same people sat at the same tables day in, day out.

The waitress brought me a glass of water and asked if I wanted a super salad. I told her I didn't really want a salad, but if it was compulsory, could I have a small salad, rather than a super one? She seemed a bit agitated and asked me again if I wanted a super salad. I explained to her that I hadn't had breakfast yet, and that the prospect of having a super-sized salad wasn't all that attractive to me. Maybe if the weather was a bit warmer it would be nice. Also, it must be said, I didn't entirely trust the American definition of salad. In the wine-growing area north of San Francisco the previous week, I had had a salad with strawberries, star fruit and marigold petals.

The waitress turned on her heel and went to fetch a man who was serving behind the counter and, I assumed, was the owner. He seemed quite concerned that I didn't want a super salad but he cheered up noticeably when he worked out that I was English. Then he started to speak slowly and the penny dropped. The question they'd been asking all along was: 'Soup or salad?' I chose neither but opted for a chicken steak, because I assumed it would be a large breast fillet, and with it came mashed potatoes, gravy, and corn. The chicken steak turned out to be a small beef steak which had been dipped in batter and deep fried. Apparently it was so-called because the steak was smothered in the same Texan batter used to fry chickens. It is a very silly dish, like deep-fried Mars bars, which annihilates all the tender, juicy qualities of a perfectly reasonable steak. I vowed then and there to avoid chicken steak like the plague.

Apocalypse any minute

I ate at many family run restaurants all over America, carefully avoiding the kind of plush establishments where pianists struggled with the 'Shadow of your Smile', and where the carpets were so thick it was impossible to hear the wine waiter, so I would jump out of my skin every time he filled up my glass. These were the types of places people would invariably recommend once they found out that I was on a mission to bring the great traditions of American food to a British audience.

In a wooden shack on the beach in St Petersburg in Florida, I was enjoying a thick white fillet of grilled grouper, a fish from the cod family that swims in the warm waters of the Gulf of Mexico. I'd been to this little café several times before in my short stay and it hadn't disappointed. I'd tried all the seafood dishes on the menu: the sweet legs of stone crabs, fresh shrimp with hot spicy sauce, and conch fritters, but the grouper was the best and it came with the finest coleslaw I'd ever tasted. It was a balmy night and I was sitting outside a shack under the stars thinking I must have a go at fishing for grouper before going back home, when I was joined by a couple of sport anglers who had pulled up in a pickup, towing a small powerboat decked out with fishing rods.

When they discovered I was English they insisted on buying me a beer and, of course, the conversation turned as always to what I was doing in America. They were called Doug (he did all the talking) and Mac, and apparently they used to be US Rangers during the Vietnam War – that's the equivalent of the SAS – and they spent most of their tour of duty fighting the Vietcong in small groups behind enemy lines, living deep in the jungles of South Vietnam. Pretty much a law unto themselves, from what I could gather. They said that when they came home they couldn't adjust back to normal life, so they and a few of their army colleagues had built their own military-style camp of trailers – mobile homes to us – on the banks of a river. I mentioned that I had joined the Territorial Army when I was eighteen and we'd go camping at weekends, but sadly they had never heard of it. They asked if it was a combat unit. The thought of combat hadn't entered my mind. To me it was more like a drinking club, which it was in those days.

They'd clearly had quite a lot to drink and in a matter of a few minutes they were asking if I wanted to go fishing with them.

I asked them what sort of fish we might catch and they said to each other, 'Shall we take him fishing for black grouper?' And then they started laughing.

I didn't know what *black* grouper were.

Or maybe, they suggested, we should fish for bonefish, because they were the best fighters. I thought it might make an interesting sequence for Keith to go out and try to catch either of these fish and cook them for these two guys, so we arranged to meet the next day at their camp by a junction on Interstate 75. Look out for the Stars and Stripes flying from the flagpole, they said.

'Ain't had so much fun since the pigs ate my little sister,' said Doug in his southern drawl, as they headed off.

It was gone eleven when I knocked at the green trailer door looking for Doug and his friend. There were about a dozen or so similar mobile homes parked with military precision around a tall flagpole. After a while Doug answered the door wearing a Japanese dressing gown. He didn't look particularly pleased to see me. Perhaps he'd forgotten about our proposed fishing trip altogether. Nevertheless, he invited me inside for coffee. The walls of the trailer were decorated with Samurai swords, hand-guns, throwing knives, and a few framed photographs of soldiers in camouflage fatigues posing in the jungle. While Doug was making the coffee I studied the pictures, hoping no one would be holding up a human head as a trophy.

After a while Doug explained that they'd had a problem with the boat I had seen them with the previous night, so they'd have to use another one; meanwhile he suggested we went for a few beers at their clubhouse. Lunchtime came and went and the empty cans started stacking up on the Formica-topped table. It became pretty clear to me that neither of these guys really wanted to go fishing that day. I could see the afternoon slipping away into a haze of stale beer and cigarette smoke, so in the nicest possible way, I explained that where I came from if someone said they would take you fishing, then a-fishing you would go.

It was late, well past two o'clock, by the time I found myself wending down the river with the almost silent Mac, Doug having preferred to stay behind and drink. We had bought a case of cold beer, and live prawns from the bar to use as bait. How did I get myself into this, I was asking myself. Mac seemed to have been born bad tempered. Not terribly reassuring, today he was looking like a character from John Boorman's film *Deliverance*, as thin as a rake with filthy denims and a straggly beard. He never once looked me in the eye. Even so, the views on the journey were a delight. I'd get quite excited at the sight of pelicans taking off in front of the boat, but Mac just grunted. Then as we motored on upstream and as the sun sank close to the tops of the ancient trees hung with moss, this crazy man started talking about the things he used to do in the Vietnam War, and I couldn't help but think about that scene towards the end of *Apocalypse Now*, when they finally go down the eerie river with bodies hanging from the trees, to find Marlon Brando's mad Colonel Walter E. Kurtz. Then the engine note changed and we started to slow down.

Mac cut the engine and showed me how to thread a live prawn on to the hook without killing it. All we had to do was drop the line over the side and let the river's current take the bait, hopefully right in front of the nose of a passing bonefish. We drank some beer and watched the line play among the eddies and little whirlpools as it made its way downstream. All the time we were being eaten alive by almost invisible stinging flies which Mac, in his prosaic way, called 'no-see-ems'. We waited for the urgent splash that would signal a bite, but none came. As it grew darker the dry reeds rustled on the riverbank. I hoped the creatures in there would be beavers and not alligators, which Mac said would start to show an interest in their surroundings at this time of day.

Deciding that the fishing might be better further upstream, my grumpy companion and I reeled in, and Mac started the engine. Other boats passed us, but always travelling in the opposite direction. Our destination turned out to be a small creek leading off the main river and as the boat made a left turn into it, all of a sudden it stopped. We'd hit a sandbank and the boat was stuck fast. I could clearly see the sandy bottom and thought of jumping over the side to push us off, but what about the alligators? Mac revved the engine mercilessly, but alas the boat refused to budge. I could smell hot metal and the engine was really shrieking, but more importantly, I could see that there was no water coming out of the side. Having had a boat myself, I knew that this was a sure indication that there was something wrong with the cooling system. I was about to mention this to Mac when there was a loud bang, followed by the tick, tick, ticking that metal makes when it is super hot – and then silence.

At a guess I reckoned there was another hour of light left in the sky and here we were, literally stuck up a creek without a paddle. Mac opened another can and told me not to worry. The guys at the camp would realise we were long overdue and come looking for us, he said. No, they wouldn't, I thought. They'd be as drunk as skunks and it wouldn't be until their hangovers wore off next morning that they would even notice we were missing. The no-see-ems kept biting and the cracking and rustling in the reed bed seemed to grow ominously louder.

By now I had lost interest in fishing and trying to make polite conversation. All I could think of was how to get safely off this boat. Then suddenly Mac put down his beer and told me to start fishing. He'd spotted a police patrol boat coming towards us. Yippee, we were saved.

'Don't even think about it,' warned Mac, very quietly. 'Keep fishing. And if they ask any questions just say everything's OK.'

One glance at his grizzled face told me he was being deadly serious. The police boat slowed and made its way towards us and as it got nearer I couldn't help noticing the bullet holes in the hull. A policeman came out of the wheelhouse and asked if we were OK.

'Sure,' said Mac, 'doing a little fishin'. We'll be off as soon as the sun sets.'

'Good luck,' waved the policeman and the patrol boat headed away upstream into the gloom as I watched, distraught.

I turned on Mac. 'Why did you let them go?'

'Because we're not supposed to have beer on-board a boat in a National Park,' he told me. 'It's strictly against the law.'

I thought, beer on-board a boat, come on! Nevertheless something about him scared me.

There were no other boats on the river. We were all alone and by now the sun had gone from the sky and we were in a world of monochrome. Funny, but when there's less to see the brain seems to overcompensate by heightening sounds. The plops and splashes grew louder and I was starting to become really scared. When I suggested to Mac that I had little faith in his friends noticing we were missing, he told me to watch what I said, because he knew his friends a lot better than I did. Not only were we stranded midstream surrounded by man-eating flies and alligators growing friskier by the minute, but I was stuck with a madman. Dear God, I said to myself, if I get out of this alive, I'll *really* give up smoking, and not cheat, even when I have a pint of beer. And the next time I make a television series I'll leave it to proper researchers and I will never, ever again get involved with complete strangers in bars late at night.

I saw the outline of the returning police boat before Mac did.

'Just say everything's fine and he'll be on his way, otherwise there's goin' to be a lot of trouble,' he told me menacingly.

I said nothing; just waited for the boat to come closer. Please say something, please say something, I willed the policemen. A voice over their loud hailer asked if we were OK. I leapt up and started to wave my blazer around my head, shouting at the top of my voice that no, we were definitely not OK. Help, help help!

'Sit down and shut up,' snarled Mac, but it was too late. The boat was heading towards us. There were two policemen on-board and the one standing in the stern asked what the problem was. In a great rush, I poured out everything: the sandbank, the engine exploding, the alligators, and the powerful yearning I had to get off this boat and return to my hotel where I would have the biggest and most potent cocktail on the menu card – note to God, sans cigarette.

The policemen pulled alongside and asked for ID. Mac didn't have his on him, which I think is an offence in these parts, whereas I had a little blue card from the BBC asking whoever should be reading it to assist me in my activities.

'What *are* your activities?' one policeman asked.

'Well, I make cookery programmes with this chef, who is incredibly charismatic, and wears a bow tie, and he loves to drink a glass of wine and catch fish and cook them, and I'm out here on a research trip,' I replied.

'So why are you out here in the middle of the river in the dark?' asked the rather incredulous policeman.

Good question I thought. *Good question.*

The other policeman was busy on the radio reading out the identification number of our boat, while Mac just glared at me with the kind of pure hatred that features heavily in the early westerns of Sam Peckinpah. Usually the look happens just before people get blown off their feet by the blasts of sawn-off shotguns, in glorious slow motion. Our fishing boat, it seemed, was stolen and it turned out my mad friend might well have been a wanted man in another state. The policemen asked Mac to join them in their boat, while I was told to sit down in the stern, and, after tying a rope to the bow, they towed me back downstream.

Any hopes I had of them escorting me safely to the camp, so I could collect my car and escape, evaporated when they dumped me on the first wooden pier they came across, telling me someone would be along to pick me up. Rather feebly I apologized to Mac for the trouble I'd landed him in. I stopped myself from pointing out that it was a good job they hadn't noticed the case of beer, otherwise he'd *really* be in trouble.

I watched the silhouettes disappear downstream against the russet-coloured sky and for the next couple of hours I was alone in the pitch dark, surrounded by the strange rustles from the riverbank, loud plops and alarming splashes from midstream, and the no-see-ems swooping in like a relentless squadron of Stukas.

All of a sudden I was dazzled by approaching car headlights. A figure stepped out of the car, and I saw, not the hoped for police officer, but Doug walking towards me. I'd just betrayed this former Vietnam vet's mate to the police; I'd virtually handed him over to them like a stuffed goose, and now he was walking menacingly towards me in the dark, in the middle of nowhere. He told me to get in the car.

'Look Doug, I can explain everything.'

'Aw, forget it,' he said. 'The guy's an asshole; had it coming. He's just a disturbed person. He walks into trouble the way people walk through doors. I'm not sorry to see the back of him.'

I found out weeks later that black grouper was a code name for boxes full of cocaine, completely sealed in black waterproof covers, that are dropped from light aircraft around the shores of Florida. They have radio beacons attached to them so that boats can go out at night and pick them up.

Be my buddy, Holly

After that escapade it was clear I needed to become more circumspect in my travels, otherwise something really dreadful would befall me. I enlisted the aid of the local Chamber of Commerce to help me find some rather less terrifying characters and locations. Accordingly, a young woman arrived at my hotel in an open-top Mustang ready to show me the sights. She was called Holly and at first glance she reminded me of Lulu; well, Lulu in a blue business suit with a cream blouse. She even had a deep raspy voice. Fortunately, she had seen a couple of the Floyd programmes on PBS – the American public service broadcasting – so she understood the criteria and wasted no time in showing me the places she loved way off the beaten track. We would stop for lunch at small beach bars and eat the claws of stone crabs with drawn butter, small, sweet-tasting oysters, fried shrimps dipped in hot sauce, blackened catfish and mullet, the freshest tasting tuna carpaccio, or huge, thick fillets of grilled swordfish. Every mouthful consumed in the company of the delightful Holly made the seafood seem even more delicious. Another time we hired a boat and fished for grouper, without any accompanying madmen and police boats, and the skipper grilled them for us on a deserted beach straight from a Bounty Bar advert. As the sun set, I began to think I had dropped into a Mills and Boon novelette.

The things I loved most about Florida were the little wooden fishing piers that jutted out to sea from seemingly every township on the Gulf of Mexico. They were the embodiment of the Declaration of Independence where everyone was given the right to life, liberty, and the pursuit of happiness. And for a brief few days, I'm ashamed to say, I pursued as much happiness as time would allow. In truth, by now, I had listed more than enough cooks, characters, fishing boats, and restaurants to fill up three programmes. The problem was I couldn't tear myself away.

'Is that enough?' Holly finally asked as we were driving back from a fishing camp.

The honourable and professional reply would have been: 'Yes thank you Holly, I've seen more than enough. You've been terrifically helpful, and I shall fly back tomorrow, because I'm missing my beautiful wife and daughter terribly.' (Did I mention that I had been married for about ten years to my second wife Judith, who was lovely, like a film star? I had met her in Hong Kong and fell hook, line, and sinker.)

Instead, I thought for a while, watching the palm trees whizzing by.

'Um, maybe tomorrow we could see a little bit more, and then that should be enough.'

'Sure,' she said, 'what have you got in mind?'

I wanted to say 'Well actually, Holly, it's you.' But instead I said, 'Hot smoked fish. I've heard about restaurants that specialize in smoking all sorts of fish over mesquite logs.'

On our last evening we were driving back to the hotel, where I had to pack before catching my plane. The sun was sinking fast and it was still very warm, and I suddenly realized I hadn't been for a swim all the time I'd been in Florida. We were driving past yet another Bounty-ad sandy beach. There was not a soul around, so I asked Holly to pull over as it would be a crying shame for me to return to chilly England without having had a dip in this beautiful warm sea.

Bashfully, I suggested she wait by the car as I'd have to swim in my underpants. Rick Stein repeatedly tells me I'm the slowest swimmer in the world, but blissfully I pootled along, feeling wonderfully cool and liberated in that silky sea. And then, as I turned round to look back at the beach, I saw her swimming towards me. Crikey, I thought, as I trod water, this is getting more like Mills and Boon by the minute.

'We've become good buddies, haven't we?' said Holly.

And then, right out of the blue, she kissed me. Clumsily, I kissed her back as best I could without sinking and then, after a few precious seconds, we swam for the shore.

Back in the car, I thought I must be the luckiest person on the planet. Here I was, travelling around with a beautiful girl, eating some of the best seafood in the world in nothing less than a tropical paradise. And I was being paid to do it. However, I suspect that at this point, if any of my left-wing film-maker friends are reading this book, they will be ripping it up in disgust and throwing it as far out of the window as humanly possible.

Anyone can be a TV cook

Floyd told me on many occasions that he hated stardom and the cult of the celebrity but I didn't believe him. The American 'recce' over, I was back in San Francisco, and we were making the programme for real. At the end of one day's filming, Floyd began telling me how his life has changed since he had been on television.

'It's terrible,' he said, 'being recognized all over the place. I can't even get on a train without some old trout coming up to me and asking how to cook partridge. You've got no idea.'

I said that I thought he was extremely lucky, because being a cook on television was a pretty cushy job compared, for example, to being a school dinner lady earning about thirty-five pounds a week.

'Cushy!' he exploded. 'You think what I do is *cushy*?'

I told him that indeed it was. He had probably one of the easiest and most delightful jobs imaginable. All he had to do was cut things up and fry them for a while or put them in a pot.

The film crew had become quite interested in this little bit of repartee and Timmy, the sound man, started to stir things up a bit.

'So you think it's easy being a cook on the telly, do you, David?' he asked.

'Well, yes, I do,' I said, determined not to give an inch. 'You get paid lots of money for doing what most people do every day of their lives. Then you write a book, which is largely based on other people's research, and make a fortune because the television series is a free advert promoting it.'

'OK, Sunshine,' said Floyd. 'Tomorrow you do the cooking and I'll do the directing, and let's see how well you get on.'

There was no getting out of this one. Keith and the crew were gleefully determined to hold me to his challenge.

And so it came to pass that on a cliff overlooking the Golden Gate Bridge, I cooked a San Franciscan clam chowder in front of the camera. It was extremely helpful that Andy MacCormack, the assistant cameraman, stood in my eyeline, wearing an apron with the recipe printed on it. Rather annoyingly Keith's directing was sure-footed and supportive as I cheerfully chirped on about all the ingredients getting to know each other in the pot. If I had to rate my performance, I would say it was a little hesitant, but quite funny.

Amazingly, the chowder was delicious. The San Francisco chowder, unlike the famous version from Boston which originated among French fishermen, is influenced by the *Italian* fishermen who arrived a century ago, and is made with tomatoes and garlic, a few potatoes, clams, and wine. I cook it to this day using fresh cockles. Afterwards, Floyd and I shook hands and decided to put the sequence into the series. I still maintain, though, that being a TV chef is a hell of a lot easier than being a school dinner lady.

PART VIII

There comes a tide in the affairs of man

I decided to leave my staff job at the BBC in Plymouth after a decision was made to take my cocktail cabinet away from me. Before that happened many journalists from the newsroom would pop in to see me with various ideas (usually abysmal) after the pubs had closed for the afternoon. Curiously, after the endless supply of free booze dried up, people stopped knocking on my door with yet another idea for a wonderful programme set in the south-west. The writing, it seemed to me, was very much on the wall. The Features Department was losing its appeal for the policy-makers who were shifting their attention more and more towards local news and current affairs.

Perhaps the life of a freelance would be more rewarding, both financially and creatively? Floyd had unceasingly tried to encourage me to form a company with him, insisting we could make a fortune filming commercials, promotional videos, and television programmes the world over. I thought long and hard. I had sleepless nights. I went for long walks, weighing everything up from all sides. What about my pension? Who would sign my expenses? Was there life after the BBC?

One day, after we'd been filming around Loch Fyne, I met up with the Scottish laird, Johnny Noble, who had founded this famous oyster fishery. Despite his tartan trousers, bonnet, and faded red fisherman's smock, he spoke with an Etonian accent, something he told me he very much regretted. However, he was the most passionate advocate of fresh seafood I had come across and his was the best smoked salmon I'd tasted. His real love affair was with the oysters that came from the loch that lapped the shore outside his stately castle. The oysters, he said, were the taste of home. As far away as Hong Kong, if he ate a Loch Fyne oyster in a restaurant, he would immediately be transported back to the green glens that swept down to his beloved loch.

After eating three dozen or so such beauties, accompanied by a couple of bottles of Muscadet, I told him about my conundrum. Should I stay or should I go?

He thought for a while and then quoted the Bard: 'There's a tide in the affairs of men. Which, taken at the flood, leads on to fortune.'

These aristos always have an elegant way of spelling things out, I thought. It was a pity I didn't know then that his piece of advice came from Julius Caesar. Had I realized, I might not have left the cosiness of the BBC on the Ides of March 1990.

The recession had just started to kick in and all the conversations Floyd and I had had about starting our own company and making lots of money came to naught. No one seemed to have the money for videos promoting their companies, and I wondered if there would still be a market for television programmes with a wine-slurping chef, come to that. Keith had just bought a pub in Devon and a new Bentley. I, meanwhile, was in a state of despair. For the first time ever I went to the supermarket with a strict shopping list. My mother's style of cooking on a shoestring budget was enjoying a renaissance at home; two lamb chops and not five, one pork chop and not three, boiled brisket instead of roast sirloin, and plaice rather than turbot. Then out of the blue, like a good genie, an offer came to discover the wonderful food of Australia in the guise of *Floyd on Oz*. It was commissioned by an Australian company, and it would also be shown on the BBC.

The first thing Floyd and I did when we arrived in Australia was go to a camping and outdoor shop and get kitted out for this gastronomic journey. Keith was always very dress conscious. In the early days, in his cavalry twills, blazers, and shirts from Jermyn Street, and his suits from Savile Row, he was like James Bond. And when we were filming all over the world, he always liked to dress like one of the natives: a beret in La Belle France, a poncho in Santa Fe, a proper handmade Stetson and cowboy boots in Texas. He was always very aware of the way he would look in front of the camera. Unlike Rick Stein, I might add, who wears only blue shirts and jeans, all the time, and makes a habit of getting his hair cut mid-shoot, leaving me with a big continuity headache.

We bought a safari suit each – easily washable, with lots of pockets – essential, we thought, if you wanted to be taken seriously in this country. Next, boots, because over here boots define who you are, and R. M. Williams boots say, 'I'm a pretty rugged type of bloke and I like having a few beers with my mates after shearing five hundred Merino sheep with one hand tied behind my back. But if anyone says anything bad about this beautiful country of mine, then I'm the nastiest bastard they're ever likely to come across in a lifetime.' They're that type of boot.

I had to have a sheath knife; after all we were going into the outback where there were lots of dangerous things, and it would also come in useful for cutting cheese and slicing tomatoes for an al fresco lunch. Finally, a hat to set off this exciting new ensemble, a hat with one side of the brim folded up in true Aussie style. We couldn't wait to get into our new clothes, and left the shop both of us dressed up like Stewart Granger from *Bhowani Junction*. Judging by the way the customers looked at us as we entered the nearest bar and ordered a couple of cold ones, they must have thought we cut a bit of a dash. One of them asked if we'd been in Australia long. I told him that we'd only just arrived, which seemed to cause a great deal of merriment.

Over the next few weeks we filmed in places where there were no settlements within a hundred miles, and no roads, so we had to arrive by light plane. At one remote fishing camp we arrived to see a huge sign warning newcomers to beware of the saltwater crocodiles or 'salties' as the locals called them. I love the way the Australians do this; postmen are posties, sunglasses are sunnies. It was blisteringly hot and I really wanted to lie down in that crystal-clear water. As if reading my mind the pilot, whose name, I think, really *was* Bruce, told me to read all the signs. The next one said, 'Don't even think about going for a swim here.'

'Understand one thing,' said Bruce. 'These crocs can outrun a horse for the first forty yards so they can easily get a hold of you.'

I thought he was being just a bit personal because I was a stone or two overweight, but he continued his welcome speech. 'They'll catch you by the leg and then drag you into the water, where they'll roll you over and over until you finally drown. And then they'll stuff you under a ledge below the water's surface, which is their larder, until you start to rot and your bloated white flesh falls easily away from the bones. That's the way they like it.'

He'd made his point. There would be no swimming for me.

We ate bush tucker and yabbies, freshwater crayfish that live in the muddy billabongs. You caught them by putting a lamb chop on the end of a piece of string. They'd pounce on it like hoodies grabbing an old lady's handbag and get hauled out of the water straight away. There was barramundi, a firm white-fleshed fish not dissimilar to bass, and in Tasmania, which is surrounded by cold water, we ate the highly prized and ultra-expensive abalone – thin slices cooked in a wok for a few seconds with a dash of oyster sauce. We also had fat white witchety grubs – huge maggots really – that tasted like cheesy scrambled eggs: not to be missed. And we ate crocodile and emu, the latter tasting heavily of blood and not something I'd want to try again in a hurry, and stews made with kangaroo tail.

We slept in curious little rooms, made out of fine steel netting, built over a square of concrete and designed to keep predators and mosquitoes at bay. They looked like my mother's meat safe, and to the local crocodile fraternity that's exactly what they were.

On one occasion we met up with a couple of cattle wranglers and their fearsome dog Alf. These tough looking blokes gathered up the strays left behind after the main round-up had taken place. Some of the cattle had been living in the outback for years and had become wise and sometimes quite dangerous. The men would build a small stockade, leaving the gate open and then, using two enormously long rolls of hessian attached to wooden posts, create two walls which got narrower and narrower, like a funnel, leading to the entrance of the stockade. They had a partner in a helicopter who would fly low so that he could herd the stray cows and steers together and drive them towards this trap.

As well as the helicopter, the wranglers had two stripped down, very quick, highly tuned Toyota Land Cruisers to help nudge the cattle between the hessian walls. They had no roofs, doors, or even seats, apart from the driver's, to make them go a bit faster. The wranglers' only protection from wild and not very willing bulls protecting their progeny were rubber tyres, hung around the vehicles like fenders on a yacht. Floyd thought this would be a wonderful chance to show off the cooking skills he had learnt while serving as a young officer in the Tank Regiment. He told me he became very popular with his men because he would cook delicious meals on the exhaust manifold of his Chieftan tank. He did this by wrapping thick, heavily seasoned steaks in tin foil with a generous splash of wine, butter, onions, and potatoes. He would cut open two or three beer cans to make a casing for this delicious ensemble, which would help protect it from the fierce heat of the tank's engine. He would then attach this metallic parcel to the manifold with wire. After driving for an hour or so – a little longer if you preferred your meat well done – his men would tuck into delicious braised steak and onions, while the other tank crews would be opening their compo rations.

Now, in the middle of the outback, he slit open a large fillet steak which he had begged from our hotel kitchen at the nearby hamlet of Fitzroy Crossing, rubbed it with garlic and seasoned it well. He then stuffed it with thinly sliced mushrooms, onions, and a generous knob of butter and fixed it on to the exhaust of the Toyota Land Cruiser, according to his trusted method. A red cloud of dust appeared on the horizon, indicating the imminent arrival of the herd. Floyd and I took our places, sitting on tyres where the passenger seats should have been, and hung on grimly as we bounced over rocks and massive anthills, narrowly missing trees.

I was convinced that the big rangy bull we were chasing knew that he and his wives and young ones were heading for a trap. He kept looking around at us, huge eyes full of fear, as if searching for a way off this roller-coaster ride.

But, alas, he and his extended family were soon inside the stockade and the gate was closed behind them. I found out later that they were going to be picked up the next day by lorry and would be sent to a factory to be turned into pet food. That news totally took the magic out of the day, and as for the steak, well, it was burnt to a crisp. Alf enjoyed it though.

Fear and loathing in Benidorm

By the time we filmed *Floyd on Spain* in 1991 I had a sense that our working relationship would soon come to an end. Keith was still very popular with viewers, and another series, *Far Flung Floyd*, was to follow, also made by an independent production company but shown on the BBC. However, we weren't getting along very well. Every three or four days during filming we'd have a row, which was tough for the film crew and took its toll on both of us. Fortunately, after every three weeks of filming we'd come home for a break, and I'd go for long solitary walks on Dartmoor. As I trudged along the stony tracks climbing higher and higher I would think about all the things that happened over the past weeks of filming, and though to my knowledge there is no history of Tourette's syndrome in my family, I found myself shouting the most terrible obscenities at the sheep.

One of the worst of the rows erupted in the holiday resort of Benidorm. I had chosen to film in this much derided resort partly because it was such a contrast to the other places we'd been to on our journey through Spain, like Galicia, Catalonia, La Mancha, and Andalusia. And also, actually, I liked it. I had come here in the early Seventies after I broke up with my first wife, Elaine. (I mentioned that my marriage, not surprisingly, didn't last very long after our short honeymoon in Ireland, didn't I?) I thought Benidorm was an honest place that wasn't trying to be anything other than what it was: cheap and cheerful. If you wanted to drink beer all day and have roast beef with gravy you could, but similarly you could swim from one of the best beaches in the whole of Spain and eat crayfish with a chilled white Rioja in a five-star hotel and it wouldn't break the bank. Also, if you travelled for barely half an hour into the hills, you could find wonderful, unspoilt villages serving great local dishes.

On that first trip, though, I did have a pretty bad experience. If you remember just one thing from reading this book then please let it be this: if you suspect an oyster to be 'off' and you have already put it in your mouth, then don't swallow it. Get rid of it immediately, even if you are halfway through an intimate conversation with the Queen. I had ordered half a dozen oysters at the bar of a pub called the Red Lion on the outskirts of Benidorm. I knew the first oyster wasn't as fresh as it should have been, but like a fool I swallowed it anyway. Fortunately I was staying at a little pension run by a kind old lady who saved my life. She gave me a nasty drink that tasted like hot petrol, and after a few sweaty, nauseous days in which I hovered between life and death, slowly I made a recovery.

When you first see Benidorm from the main highway it looks like a mini version of Chicago, with its tall skyscraper hotels huddled together on the bay. The chaps from the local tourist authority, whom we had contacted looking for interesting local things to film, were understandably suspicious of media types from Britain, whom they imagined would go out of their way to paint the town in a tacky light. Miguel from the local authority took me to a small restaurant right in the heart of the old part of town.

'No tourists come to this place,' he told me. 'They prefer chicken and chips and bottles of Cava in the cafés near the beach.'

An old lady brought a sizzling paella dish full of brown-coloured rice, so hot from the oven it was making crackling noises like a bowl of Rice Krispies.

'This is called *arroz a la banda*,' Miguel told me, scooping a huge spoonful of the sticky brown mixture, peppered with purple squid tentacles, on to my plate. 'The name means rice, cooked with anything you happen to have. It's a poor person's dish. The food of old Benidorm from the days when it was a little sleepy fishing village. Today it is rice with fresh squid.'

It was possibly one of the best rice dishes I've ever eaten and the chilled bottle of Tempranillo washed it down beautifully. Even with the passing of time I can still taste the deep, intense flavour of the special Bomba paella rice cooked slowly in good fish stock. Apparently the local saying was that 'The rice drinks the stock until she can drink no more, then it's time for her to sleep in the oven for ten minutes before she comes to the table in all her glory.' It was so good that I asked if we could have another one.

After lunch Miguel took me to a café by the beach where over strong coffees, we discussed things to film and he entertained me by detecting the nationalities of the men who strolled by, simply by what they wore.

Well-pressed shorts, matching tennis shirts, white socks, and expensive trainers meant they were German; tight Speedo swimming trunks, gold medallions, and cashmere sweaters draped over the shoulders denoted Italians. The French favoured pastel colours and expensive shoulder bags.

'How do you tell the English?' I said, although I thought I already knew the answer.

'Easy,' he said. 'You look for clothes that don't match each other, bald heads, and tattoos. Also, you are the only nation in the world to wear socks with sandals.'

Miguel asked if I liked paella and I told him it was in my top ten greatest dishes of the world, though I might have to review that after eating the delicious *arroz a la banda*. He told me that on special occasions here, they would make a paella in a massive metal pan so large that it could easily feed 2,000 people, and that the quality of the cooking was unbeatable. He said he could arrange for such a monster paella to be created in a housing estate on the outskirts of the town where most of the hotel workers lived.

'This would be a special treat for them, and a wonderful opportunity for you and your camera crew.'

I didn't hestitate. In fact I'd already started to film the crane that was lifting the huge stainless steel pan – the size of a small municipal ice rink – on to a pile of logs, when Keith turned up with his (third) wife Shaunagh in their chauffeured limousine.

I was about to introduce them to Miguel when Keith declared, 'If you think I'm going to have anything to do with *that*,' he gestured towards the men who were lighting the fire beneath the massive pan. 'You can think again. It's a travesty. Ask yourself, David,' his burning gimlet eyes boring into mine, 'how can anything cooked on this scale taste good?'

I was lost for words.

'The thing is with you, David, you know nothing about food. You're just in it for the spectacle.'

And then they were gone. I explained to Miguel that poor old Keith had had a serious bout of food poisoning and had to rush off because he couldn't be too far away from the bathroom. Of course, he would come back when he felt better.

Meanwhile, the cooking of this incredible dish had commenced. Gallons of olive oil were poured into the pan, and when it was hot, sacks of chopped garlic were thrown in and moved about with long wooden rakes by men in white overalls standing on top of ladders. When the garlic had lost its creamy whiteness and was about to turn pale gold they threw in two huge sacks of chopped duck breasts. This was followed by an equal quantity of rabbit pieces, then several sacks of jewel-like snails with black and white shells. Miguel told me the snails were gathered from the mountains, where they feed off wild herbs, mainly fennel and wild thyme, and they were highly revered by the local people. This was opera; full of life and colour and so Mediterranean, and I wished Keith could have been here to see what tremendous care was going into the dish. The men threw in armfuls of wild herbs and then scurried up and down the ladders like mechanical puppets from an old Homepride commercial from the Seventies, tipping sacks full of rice into the paella. They made sure that each grain was coated in the oil and then added powdered saffron.

The aroma of garlic, saffron, and duck aroused the curiosity of the locals and by midday they had formed a queue which was growing longer by the minute. There wasn't a bald head, shell suit, or tattoo in sight. Finally, once the stock had been added by the bucketful, everyone knew that in half an hour, when the rice had drunk just enough of the stock to make her swell beautifully, that glorious paella would be ready.

In Floyd's absence I was elected to sample the first serving, piled high on a plastic plate. I proclaimed it '*Muy bueno*' and when the assembled crowd seemed to be looking for more reassurance, I added a robust '*Delizioso*' which is actually Italian, and finally '*Brillianto*', which wasn't really anything at all.

The cooks poured me a glass of rough red wine and then started to serve the long line of people who'd been watching and waiting. I wanted to find Keith and bring him here so that he could sample the dish before it had been devoured. So leaving the crew to enjoy some of the paella and a well-deserved glass of wine, I jumped in a cab and raced off to his hotel.

I knew the moment I saw Keith and Shaunagh drinking at the pool bar that this was a mistake. Nevertheless, I blundered in.

'It's a brilliant paella, Keith,' I said. 'And if we go now you'll be able to try some. There's hundreds of people eating it and they all really seem to like it.'

Shaunagh glared at me like an angry buzzard and I felt like a field mouse considering a last minute dash for the hedgerow as Keith announced, 'I don't want to work with you any more, Pritchard. As far as I'm concerned that monstrous excuse for a paella is the last straw. I've had it with you and all your stupid ideas. I'll never be taken seriously if I carry on working with you and I'm fed up to the back teeth with people asking me how many glasses of wine I drink when I'm cooking on the television. I want to change it all.'

The ice made a dull thunk as he drained the last of his double Scotch and our meeting was over. Well and truly over, actually, after I told him he was a useless tosser, or words to that effect, and left.

'Where do you want to go, sir?' asked the taxi driver.

'*To el mucho grande paella,*' I replied, not quite sure of where it was I was headed.

'*El mucho grande paella.*' He repeated it a couple of times, tapping his fingers on the steering wheel and accentuating each word. '*El mucho grande paella.*'

I thought at any moment he was going to start singing it to the tune of 'Viva España'. He asked if I liked paella, and when I said I did, very much, he suggested taking me to his brother-in-law's restaurant where they made an especially nice one. It took a great deal of comedy Spanish to convince him that I didn't want to *eat* a paella, but *look* at one, and a giant one at that. He was still struggling with this slightly surreal thought, when I recognized one of the streets I'd travelled along earlier in the day and eventually we retraced my steps to where the film crew waited alongside a very large, empty paella dish.

A local man, no doubt cashing in on the fact that the paella had long since vanished, had started to grill small black puddings over a brazier, which he served with a hunk of bread for a few pesetas, and which the crew and I ate accompanied with cheap wine in plastic cups. It was a delicious combination and the bloody, sweet, spicy sausages made the thin Spanish hooch taste like Gevrey Chambertin, so I had rather a lot of both. By the time I arrived back at the hotel later that evening I was very drunk. When I got to my room the phone was ringing and when I answered I heard the West Country burr of Keith's agent, John Miles.

'David,' he said, making my name sound like two words. 'I've just had a chat with Keith and he's asked me to phone you.'

'Oh yeah,' I said. 'He's not by any chance thinking of jumping from his balcony, is he? Because I could go outside and cheer him on.' I thought I was being very witty.

'Now, now David. Keith is very sorry about today and really wants to apologize to you for giving you such a bad time.'

Am I dreaming this? I thought.

'He wants to apologize personally to you and would like you to go to his suite where he's expecting you.'

There was a pause while I took this in.

'John, I can't believe this. The bloke is a total moron!'

'No, no, David,' he cut in. 'He's deeply sorry and very sensitive to the situation, and wants to patch things up so you can carry on working together.'

So, after splashing my face with cold water, I found myself ringing the bell of Keith's penthouse suite. He came to the door smoking a cigarette and wearing nothing but a bath towel wrapped round his waist.

'If I've called at a bad time, I could pop back later,' I said, as if we were starring in a very bad sitcom.

'My dear chap, come in. Have a drink.'

How could this be happening? I thought, as he poured me an extremely large whisky.

And then I heard myself say: 'Sorry about today.'

'*You're* sorry?' he said, with all the authority of a Shakespearian actor. 'Dear boy, it's *I* who should apologize to *you.*'

And so we passed a very pleasant hour together talking about the future and his desire to be taken seriously as a chef. I suspect this is a pretty well-trodden path in the world of television along which the comic actor decides he wants to become a serious one, and in the middle of this hopeless transition there are tears and tantrums.

Keith asked if I planned to use the footage of the giant paella and I told him I did. And so, in the spirit of reconciliation and bonhomie, we did what we did best and concocted a plan to write a voice-over, in the no-nonsense Delia Smith style of cookery.

The scenario Keith would paint would be of someone coming home after a hard day at the office and having to prepare a little dinner party for a few friends. 'So, start off by peeling five thousand cloves of garlic, and then nip into the garden and strangle about eight hundred ducks. Don't be too fussy with the amounts at this stage. Then while you're out with the dog try and pick around twenty thousand plump snails, give or take a hundred or so.' We laughed so much we nearly fell off our chairs.

Ten years later I found out that this sudden change of heart on Keith's part wasn't genuine at all. John Miles, his wily agent, had called Keith to say that he'd received a call from *me* and that I'd admitted to behaving abominably and wished with all my heart to atone for my behaviour earlier in the day. This, of course, was music to Keith's ears, so all John had to do, to complete the trap, was to make that phone call assuring me that Keith was anxious to apologize for his appalling behaviour, and let the egos do the rest. The moral of the story, I suppose, is never underestimate an agent.

The end is nigh

Far Flung Floyd which we filmed in 1992, was to be the last series Keith and I made together. Curiously, although we had our fair share of bad patches, filming had been reasonably pleasant. Floyd, on form, was great company. We stayed in some rather splendid hotels and ate delicious local food. We filmed in Vietnam, Malaysia, and Thailand and on the island of Koh Samui, in the south of that country. It was here that Floyd told me that he had met a pirate, a real live Thai pirate. And he was holidaying with his wife and children in the hotel.

'But pirates don't go on holiday, Keith,' I said, trying to imagine Long John Silver on a sun lounger.

'That's where you're wrong. Pirating is a business like any other and when he's made enough money he goes on his holidays and takes his wife and kids,' Keith explained with great conviction.

When we'd finished filming for the day we'd go for a swim and afterwards drink pina coladas made with fresh coconut milk from the trees surrounding the pool, then tuck into huge barbecued prawns, fillets of freshly landed fish, or exquisite curries which would be made in front of us. Floyd had been exceptionally cheerful for nearly a week now and it was at the poolside bar that he introduced me to his new friend the pirate. I must admit, he did look the part. He was swarthy, with a black goatee, and he wore many gold chains around his muscular neck. I'd heard horrifying tales about Thai pirates being utterly ruthless, especially to the poor boat people fleeing Vietnam after the war.

'Mister Floyd tells me you're a real Thai pirate,' I found myself saying, trying to keep any hint of trepidation out of my voice.

'Yes thass rye, maybe for neary twenny years now,' he said in an attractive sing-song voice.

Blimey, I thought, maybe pirating isn't against the law over here. He's so relaxed and open about it and he's been doing it for twenty years. I'm sure Blackbeard and Captain Kidd didn't last that long before they were tracked down by the Royal Navy and hanged.

Floyd had a 'see I told you so' smile on his face.

'So where do you do your pirating? Anywhere around Koh Samui?' I asked.

'No,' he laughed, flashing a couple of gold teeth. 'Not *here*. Bangkok.'

I pressed him further. 'So, from Bangkok, where do you go to do your pirating?'

'Maybe Paris or New York. Sometime I go other way to Austraria and San Francisco.'

That's a bloody long way to go pirating, I thought. And then in a delicious moment I realized. He wasn't a Thai *pirate*, he was a Thai *pilot* working for Thai Airways.

Over the following weeks endless pirate jokes were bandied about, and good humour prevailed throughout the rest of the shoot. I decided to invent old proverbs to break up the cooking sequences; for example, when we filmed a family of chickens pecking the ground around Floyd's feet, he would say, 'There is an old Thai saying that goes back many centuries and that is, "the chicken that pecks the grated coconut from under the cook's table is not long for the pot."'

Keith, however, had decided that he no longer wished to be seen drinking a glass of wine while he was cooking. He said people weren't taking him seriously. So no more quick slurps. Despite the proverbs, I felt the humour wasn't coming through, and he had become a bit like a talking recipe book. The frayed elastic band that bound us together for so many years had finally snapped, and it was time to go our separate ways.

PART IX

The world of Rick Stein

After a taste of freelancing I decided I didn't like it that much after all, and so I had joined Denham Productions, a small company that made programmes for local television companies in the south-west of England. Chris Denham, the founder, is a much-loved character in the region, because for years he presented the local news programme, *Spotlight*, for the BBC. I thought it would be terrific for the future of the company if I could get a network series on the BBC for Denham Productions. I'd met many budding TV chefs over the years, including Gary Rhodes, who we filmed with Keith during *Floyd on Britain and Ireland*. Rhodes was creating great English dishes like braised oxtail at the Castle Hotel in Taunton, but, talented as he was, his style wasn't for me. The almost embarrassingly good-looking Jean-Christophe Novelli had started out working for Keith Floyd at his pub, the Maltsters Arms, in Tuckenhay. He had a repertoire of extravagant desserts which really impressed Keith, among them the shortly to be famous Jack-in-the-box, out of which popped gold springs made from spun sugar. He was clearly very talented, but I would have preferred a nicely cooked apple pie with custard.

Rick Stein, on the other hand, was different. I had first met Rick years before, while making the first series with Keith, *Floyd on Fish*. Sue King, a journalist from the BBC in Plymouth, had dropped in to my office to say she had just interviewed Rick on the local *Spotlight* programme, because his restaurant had won a recent award, and she found him really engaging. Not only did he cook fish beautifully, but he had a great mind and was incredibly well read, with a love of poetry, especially Thomas Hardy. She said he'd be good on television. The timing was perfect because Keith had caught a huge pike on the Somerset Levels and I was looking for a place for him to cook it. What's more, Keith had known Rick for some time, as he often went to Padstow where Rick and his wife Jill owned The Seafood Restaurant. Rick was in awe of Keith, because he had cooked for French people in France, and, in fact, it was Floyd who had taught him how to make an authentic bouillabaisse. On the day we filmed, Keith ended up poaching the pike in Rick's restaurant kitchen.

Floyd was bang on form, and for some reason kept calling Rick 'Nick'. I left in the sequence where Rick corrected him and they made a huge joke of it, Keith slapping Rick on the back and saying: 'Well, dear boy, when you've seen one cook, you've seen them all.'

After filming, Rick made us all a memorable steak and chips with a salad of tomatoes and red onions – it was the first time I had tasted a red onion – and we drank Beaujolais and Côtes du Rhône. I remember talking to Rick the entire time; until I noticed Floyd, sitting smoking, and looking at me balefully.

When I looked back on that clip it was clear that Rick didn't have Floyd's confidence in front of the camera. By contrast there was a kind of self-doubt, simplicity and honesty about him that he still retains today. I think this is one of the attributes that not only enchants the viewers, but makes him enduringly good company. And he's turned out to be, well, my other best friend, really.

It was the early spring of 1993 when I drove down to Padstow to meet him and talk about the prospect of making a TV series. Stupidly, I had chosen a bank holiday weekend, the restaurant was packed, and he was working flat out cooking lunches when I arrived. The kitchen smelt wonderfully of butter and tarragon and hot shellfish. There were around a dozen people grilling lobsters, filleting fish, making sauces, and creating elaborate piles of raw seafood on beds of sweet-smelling seaweed. Rick himself was cooking on a salamander, an aptly named monster of a grill, so hot the fish would buckle and bend and finally blister. No matter where I stood I kept getting in the way. Rick looked relieved when I said I'd see him later after things had quietened down, and went outside for a walk around Padstow.

I wandered through the narrow streets past shops selling fudge, freshly baked Cornish pasties, and hand lines for catching mackerel. Small boys pulled up crabs from the muddy water of the inner harbour. I felt like I was on holiday. Everything that surrounded me had a shape and scale, texture and colour that pleased the eye and lifted the spirits. A pint of bitter was called for.

The London Inn smelt of polish, tobacco, and beer, a combination of smells that has long since disappeared from the beloved British pub. It had a distinct nautical flavour, with pieces of brass from old boats dotted around the place. You could have shot a scene for a film set in the Forties without changing an ashtray. I sat in the corner with my pint and listened to the hushed conversation of a group of fishermen at the bar. Apparently, a fishing boat on its way back to the harbour had grounded at the mouth of the estuary and heavy seas had tipped it over drowning all on-board. It might have been a conversation from a hundred years ago yet this was 1993, and fishermen were still losing their lives at sea. There was something so stoical and proud about these men with weather-beaten faces, in their sailing caps and sea boots, that made me feel like a guilty outsider for not having to risk my life day in, day out, in all sorts of weather, to bring home a few boxes of fish.

I made my way back to see Rick, hoping the restaurant would be less frenetic. Some of the cooks were starting to clean up the kitchen and the hot salamander had stopped breathing fire on to fillets of turbot and Dover soles. Rick asked his second in command, Paul Ripley, to take over and suggested we went for a pint. He was still wearing his chef's whites when we walked through the door of the London Inn. The same fishermen were still there and greeted him warmly.

'Hello Ricky. Are you looking for any crabs?'

'Sure, why not, Johnny. Just bring 'em up to the restaurant and we'll take the lot.'

Over our pints Rick talked about his love for Padstow, although he wouldn't presume to call himself a local. Originally from Oxford, he had spent every holiday here as a child and when he left Oxford University, where he studied English, he decided to settle here.

He had learned to cook at the Great Western Hotel at Paddington Station, but he left because he was homesick for Cornwall. Originally he and his wife Jill had started up a nightclub. He fancied himself as his namesake played by Humphrey Bogart in the classic movie *Casablanca*. To qualify for a food licence he used to serve Vesta curries: dehydrated offerings from a packet, which, mixed with hot water and simmered for a few minutes, could be surprisingly tasty, providing whoever was going to eat them had a few beers beforehand.

'The only trouble with the club,' he explained, glancing over his shoulder at his friends by the bar, 'was that there would be monumental fights between the local fishermen and the holidaymakers. The fishermen used to come into the club after the local pubs had closed, and, of course, being red-blooded boys, they would try to chat up the women who were having innocent fun dancing with their husbands and boyfriends. The police used to call the place Dodge City and I was hospitalized three times with concussion, once when someone hit me over the head with an iron bar.'

Eventually, he said, the police decided they had had enough and the magistrates agreed, so they closed the place down. So there he was busted flat in Padstow, not knowing what to do next.

One day, he told me, he and Jill had gone to Falmouth to a little restaurant they had heard about, that was no bigger than a sweet shop. It was called Mark's Seafood Bar. Mark Righton did the cooking and his wife

Caroline served the customers. When Rick and Jill peered inside it was packed with customers who all looked like retired admirals, solicitors, or the magistrates who had closed him down. The little place had a terrific atmosphere and the food was really simple: moules marinière, grilled Dover sole, crab salad, fillets of sea bass and chips, whatever fish was caught fresh that day. It was then that he remembered he still had the food licence. And so, drawing on his experience of cooking at the Great Western, he and Jill opened The Seafood Restaurant.

We talked all that afternoon over pints of Tinners Ale. I ended up staying the night at the Stein family home, since, being a bank holiday, all the guest houses and hotels were full. Jill made me feel very welcome as did Chalky, their Jack Russell, and their three boys, Eddie, Jack, and Charles. I couldn't help but think that this was the start of a brand new adventure.

Early the next morning Rick and I took Chalky for a walk along the banks of the Camel estuary. This was the first time I'd seen this stunning vast stretch of yellow sands and turquoise water. Across the river were sand dunes and above them the bent witch's hat of St Enodoc's church spire where Sir John Betjeman lies buried. We talked about Betjeman's poetry and how it evokes memories of distant childhood – 'sand in the sandwiches, wasps in the tea' as he so aptly put it.

Rick pointed to a sandbar that seemed to stretch right across the mouth of the estuary. It was, he said, the infamous Doom Bar, and I recalled hearing the name spoken softly by the fishermen in the London Inn the previous afternoon. Many a boat had foundered on this deceiving bank of sand, he said, and it had been the cause of numerous deaths among the Padstow fishing community. Almost every family had at some time been cursed by this sleeping monster.

We walked a long way over the wet sand talking about our favourite food. His turned out to be a roasted tranche of turbot with hollandaise and Jersey Royals, whereas mine was roast beef, Yorkshire pudding, and roast potatoes. Oh, and runner beans, if they were in season. Over the booming surf we could see a few boats coming back on the incoming tide. A couple of the fishermen held up huge fish, bigger than dustbin lids, as if they were trophies.

'Bloody hell,' said Rick, 'that's fantastic. Two really big turbot.' He gave the thumbs up to the fishermen and shouted at the top of his voice that he'd buy everything they'd got.

Until that moment I hadn't really been sure what this television series would be about, should we be lucky enough for the BBC to commission it. But now I saw it clearly. It would simply capture the world of Rick Stein: Cornwall, the sea, the fishing community, the town of Padstow, fish cookery, John Betjeman's poems, Chalky the Jack Russell, and Rick's family. We would call it *A Taste of the Sea*. It would be about the Doom Bar, and the fishermen who went out in the day boats, then rolled up in their rusty old cars and vans to bring huge buckets of fish to the door of Rick's kitchen. There might be skate, dogfish, red mullet, lemon soles, hake, gurnard, scallops, or beautiful line-caught sea bass: who knew? It was like taking delivery of a great big surprise package from Hamley's toyshop every day.

'The programme has to have the smell of the sea,' said Rick, warming excitedly to the idea as we walked back. 'And the cooking's got to look good and be simple to follow. It's got to evoke everything that's great about a British seaside holiday. And it has to be true to the people of Padstow. Nobody knows the lives these fishermen lead at sea.'

Now all I had to do was write a synopsis that would impress a commissioning editor and shoot a camera test to make sure that Rick would be good on television.

Pitching an idea for a programme with an unknown presenter can be a heart-wrenching process. The last three series with Floyd, though made by outside production companies, had been happily snapped up by the BBC, because Keith was a known quantity. But now I found myself, for the first time since I had left my job at the BBC, looking in on the workings of the Corporation from the outside, knowing that commissioning editors come and go and that the proposal I spent days writing would most likely slide to the bottom of in trays like sediment in a bottle of port. I'd phone up to ask for the thoughts of the commissioning editor of the moment, but invariably I'd be automatically transferred to the answerphone. Most of all I dreaded being on the receiving end of the classic excuses I knew so well, such as, 'We're very interested but we're looking for slots later in the year', which really meant, 'forget it'.

In the meantime we made a tape featuring Rick buying fish off the boats at Padstow and cooking it in his restaurant. It wasn't very good, mainly because we were all trying too hard. I blamed myself. Rick is a naturally quiet and philosophical person, with a wry sense of humour, a great passion for food, and a love of Cornwall. But none of this was coming across. Perhaps inadvertently I was trying to make him be someone he wasn't. Maybe I was so used to Keith Floyd being (in the early days at least) so easily ebullient, so funny. No matter how I edited this tape, I knew that to submit it to the BBC would be counterproductive.

A week or so later we tried again. I'd arranged to meet Rick on the outer pier at Padstow because this time we would go out to sea with a local fisherman. I was nervous. This reshoot had to work because I was conscious that this might be my last chance. I had to find a way of unlocking the limitless passion I knew that Rick had for his subject. I was deep in thought as I walked from my car when I was approached by Jim Sprowle, a fish merchant, who had at one time been Keith Floyd's brother-in-law.

'I hear you're planning to do the same thing with Rick as you did with Keith,' he said.

I told him that the two characters were like chalk and cheese, but yes it was true I wanted to put Rick on the television and to show people a glimpse of his world.

'It'll never work,' he said. 'Rick's too shy. I've known him for years and he's too quiet and reserved. Don't get me wrong, he's a lovely bloke an' all that, but he won't work on the telly.'

Thanks very much, I thought, that's all I need.

I didn't mention Jim's comments to Rick and undaunted by the spectre of failure, we went out to sea in a small, very rocky, crab boat. Rick talked to the camera about fishing in Cornwall and when we arrived back, we filmed some more on the quayside. But he looked tortured and I realized I'd cocked it up again. It was as if Rick was trying to please me by putting over a louder and more flamboyant version of his natural personality. In other words, he was trying to be a Television Presenter, when in fact he was so much better than that.

I'd arranged to show Rick the camera test at our offices on the docks in Plymouth a week later, and I was dreading it. It was late afternoon and the low sunlight was beautiful, turning the water of the River Plym into molten gold, and I wished we could give it one more go in this lovely light. Then, as if in answer to my prayers, Colin Rowe, a cameraman and director of the company, drove into the small car park with his sound recordist Zyna Haskell-Brown, having finished filming somewhere else. I asked Rick if he would be willing to give it another try, but this time I wanted to see the bloke I had met in the pub all those weeks ago, talking, as compellingly as he had done then, about his life in Cornwall. He sat down on a rusty old bollard and while Colin filmed he talked to me in a soft, unhurried voice about his love of cooking and of Padstow. He described his world: the light on the estuary, the great characters who supplied him with fish, the fussy customers. It was like listening to a Cornish version of *Under Milk Wood*. When I feel things are going really well I tend to steal a glance at the sound recordist to see their expression as they monitor the words. If they're smiling, then I know we're going to be OK. Zyna was beaming.

At last I had the complete package. Both Rick and I were bursting with optimism and couldn't wait to get out on location and start filming. It was impossible to think about anything else. Every time the telephone rang my heart beat faster, but it was never the right call. Months went by and another commissioning editor, Jeremy Gibson, took over the role. He was very sympathetic, but still we had to wait. Apparently the bosses at the BBC couldn't quite make up their minds whether to go with a series based on a chef from Bath, or Rick Stein.

During that tense time Rick and I would meet up every few months in the London Inn in Padstow, where we mapped out the whole of the series we wanted to make, trying to remain optimistic. I wondered whether we would have remained friends if the BBC turned us down. I'd like to think so.

Then one day I received a call from Rick. Michael Grade, who was at that time the chief executive of Channel 4, had been in the restaurant the previous night and Rick had joined him and his guests for a drink before they left. He told him about our filming and our plans and how frustrating he thought this whole television business was. Of course, he was talking to the consummate broadcasting chief, who knew more than anyone how this labyrinthine industry works. I had no idea whether Michael had any interest in commissioning the series himself, but Lew Grade, his uncle, once famously said about the television industry, 'Caste your bread upon the waters and with any luck it'll come back as smoked salmon sandwiches.' This was the impetus I needed to make a last ditch attempt at getting a positive answer out of the BBC.

I left a message on Jeremy Gibson's answerphone saying that there was a really strong possibility that the idea would go to Channel 4 as, unbeknown to me, Rick was really good friends with Michael Grade, who thought the whole idea utterly brilliant. My gambit worked, because a day later we got the go ahead to proceed.

Filmingland

Because Rick and I are good friends and enjoy working together so much, when we make TV programmes it's a bit like, as he says, 'We're going off on holiday to Filmingland.' Our crew, Chris Topliss, on camera, Pete Underwood on sound, and Arezoo Farahzad, my new Iranian Frances, has been together for twelve years and they are like family to me. I love them to bits; so it's as if we all go off together and eat lots of food and have lots of fun going to jungles and markets and out on boats, and, well, we may as well film it and then we can take it back and show it to people. There are moments when we just think, 'We are so lucky.'

I'd like to say that everything fell magically into place from the beginning. However, the first day's filming was an utter, utter disaster. I had an excellent cameraman, Julian Clinkard, and the pictures were glorious, but Rick had just recovered from glandular fever, and there was no life, no spark in him. I was getting no goosebumps, no excitement, no hint of magic. He was just … flat. The conger eels, scallops, and mussels that were also in the scene positively glistened by comparison. You have to be an optimist, so I carried on filming but as we packed up the equipment and started loading the vehicles no one was saying, 'Hey, day one, not bad … what's the call time tomorrow?' Or, 'Fancy a pint?' Or, 'I really liked that dish, Rick, I wouldn't mind the recipe for that.' There was just a silence.

I was thinking I might have to phone the BBC and say, 'Look, you know I asked for six programmes with Rick Stein, well what about one? Or half of one.'

I sat on the bonnet of my car feeling dejected. Perhaps, after all, Rick didn't have the power to connect the viewer to his world in the way that Keith had done so effortlessly.

Sensing my mood, a good friend of mine, Maggie, who had come along to watch the filming, came over and said: 'You have to believe in him, David. You have to believe in the chap you love listening to in the pub, who can talk for hours about his love of fish and how to cook it, about Cornwall and the fishermen.'

'I know that,' I said. 'But where is he?'

For some reason I had with me *The Faber Book of Food* and, more to distract myself from my problem than anything else, I happened to flip it open, and there was a recipe in there for Crab Newburg, written by an American woman, Marjorie Kinnan Rawlings, in 1942. She made the dish with cream from her Jersey cows and as I started to read it I was struck by how beautifully she described cooking and eating it. She ended by saying, 'My friends rise from the table, wring my hand with deep feeling, and slip quietly and reverently away. I sit alone and weep for the misery of a world that does not have blue crabs and a Jersey cow.' As it turned out, Marjorie was to be my salvation.

I took Rick to the pub. It was time to be truthful, but not in front of a film crew. You will never get a performance that way.

I showed the book to Rick and I said, 'Forget about cooking, I want you to read this, out on the cliffs overlooking the estuary where the water is that stunning shade of aquamarine, better than Walt Disney could ever make it. Then we'll illustrate your words with close-ups of the crab, the cream ... and I want you to wear your chef's whites.'

The thing about being a director is that, actually, secretly, you really want to be in front of the camera and not behind it. I could see myself cooking paella, risotto, and jambalaya, all the while talking passionately about what I was doing, but the reality is, I'm no chef, and I don't have the authority of a Keith Floyd or Rick Stein. So it's a pipe dream, really, but this feel for performing, or showing off, as my daughter Lucy calls it, is extremely helpful when you are directing, particularly when things are not going well.

So the next morning Rick sat out on the cliff and he read this extract, and in that one shot I saw what the viewer at home would see: a lovely, quiet, modest man, with a real emotional connection to this part of the world. No, he wasn't like Keith Floyd, a showman in bow ties and blazers, glass of wine in hand: roll up, roll up and we'll all go to the fair. But that was actually a plus, not a minus. And that was how we progressed, step by step.

In the afternoon, I said to Rick: 'Tell people about the Doom Bar.'

And he started talking about this bank of sand that controlled the lives of everyone around Padstow. He talked about the way the sea would go down and the boats would get stuck on the sand. Then the waves would come in, tip the boats over, and the people would fall out and inevitably drown. A few months previously, he said, four boys he had known all their lives had drowned. As he was talking about this community he was so in tune with, and cared so much about, his face changed. I thought for a minute he was going to cry. I actually felt quite tearful myself. I was getting amazing material here, so much more than just a cookery programme.

We went back to Rick's home to carry on filming, and while he was sitting on the sofa talking to me about his life, Chalky suddenly looked at the microphone on the end of the pole and apparently found it incredibly threatening, so he started to growl. Rick was talking, and Chalky was growling.

'Should I carry on?' Rick asked, trying not to laugh.

Then suddenly Chalky leapt up as if to attack the microphone. It was so funny I nearly fell off my chair laughing; one of those brilliant moments that has been shown again and again on TV since. From then on Chalky came with us everywhere we went; even if it meant smuggling him into hotels inside an overnight bag. A local fisherman, Brian Bate, said that Chalky had become even more famous than Rick, and I think it was probably true.

Looking back I don't really know what went wrong that first day. No one wanted to rake over the smoky ruins. With television very often the joy that comes with getting a commission is superseded by a dark cloud of seriousness once you start filming. Maybe the cloud descended that day, and Rick, being on the front end of things, had simply found himself thinking: 'Can I really do it?' We never intellectualized the problem, because suddenly it all started going right. In the space of two days we had gone from total despair to utter jubilation.

The odd couple

The television world is full of jealousies and insecurities, and when you work closely with someone I often think it is a bit like being in a marriage. Frankly I would get very upset if Rick were to go off and film with someone else for any length of time. I would hope that the camera wouldn't work and the director would be utterly incompetent. I've had lots of offers, but if I was to start working with another chef, I know for a fact Rick wouldn't like it. It would be bloody bad manners. Like a chap taking on a mistress. You really shouldn't do it.

Actually, forget the old married couple idea, we're really more like Walter Matthau and Jack Lemon in that brilliantly funny movie, *The Odd Couple*. We can both be seriously cranky and bad tempered at times, especially when trapped together, filming on a barge for two months, but it's all part of the fun.

Sometimes, when you are making television programmes, you have to do an awful lot of research, but what Rick and I would do was go to the pub and have a chat. The London Inn in Padstow became a sort of melting pot out of which would always come a filming schedule.

Rick would say, 'We're getting some great grey mullet at the moment' and I would tell him I never liked grey mullet much. They were so plentiful when I was a child they would turn the tributary of the River Itchen black. We kids would get broom handles, tie toasting forks to the end of them, then wade in and stab these poor fish. Nobody wanted to eat them because they were thought to gobble up the mud and effluent from the sewage pipes, so we'd end up feeding them to our cat. But Rick would disagree, and say that grey mullet, especially when caught out at sea, was as good as bass, if not better. The next evening, as the sun sank, we would be out in a rowing boat in the silky pink evening light, catching spankingly fresh, silvery grey mullet that were nothing like the derided fish of my childhood. Then Rick would cook them, and, of course, they tasted wonderful. He was right, definitely as good as bass.

The following day we'd go to the pub again, and we'd meet another fisherman who was going out for turbot the following morning, so we'd say, 'Thank you very much.'

And so it went on. I don't remember ever typing up a proper schedule with call times and plans for the day. It was more like a phone call to the crew: 'The boat leaves at six in the morning. Be on it.'

And nothing much has changed really. Sometimes I think, if I was teetotal, I couldn't do this job.

Like Jack and Walter we know all of each other's little foibles. Very often Rick accuses me of digging a big hole for myself and everyone else around me, totally unnecessarily. He calls it the 'Bouillabaisse Situation'. We were researching around Marseilles, trying to find the best bouillabaisse. Eventually, after days of eating nothing but bouillabaisse, we booked into a hotel further along the coast in Cassis, and the man at the desk asked, 'Will you be staying for dinner?'

'Yes we will,' I said. 'But, the thing is this: we don't want bouillabaisse. We have had bouillabaisse for breakfast, bouillabaisse for lunch, bouillabaisse for dinner, bouillabaisse for supper. So no bouillabaisse. Anything but bouillabaisse.'

I could see Rick's eyes looking up at the ceiling. And sure enough when we came down for dinner, what happened? While all around us people were tucking into lovely looking langoustines and steaks, nobody brought us a menu. Instead, out came a big bowl of bouillabaisse for two.

'You see,' remonstrated Rick. 'That's what you do. You always have to dig a big hole; you over-explain, over-elaborate, over-insist, and now you've got us stuck with bouillabaisse again.'

So now, whenever I'm talking to someone and he thinks I'm digging us into another hole, I hear a low muttering in the background: 'bouillabaisse, bouillabaisse …'.

He, on the other hand, can be the most cantankerous person you've ever met. Once we were having supper with Bill Baker, the wine merchant, who is sadly no longer with us, and Simon Hopkinson, probably one of the best cooks and food writers ever, and we got to talking about Cornish pasties. Now Rick prides himself on the Cornish pasties he makes at his delicatessen in Padstow. It's a very sensitive subject and Cornish people get extremely touchy and precious about what should go into a pasty. Personally, I think it should be potato, swede, onion, and shin of beef – definitely no carrots. Then, when you get on to the subject of pastry, it's a more contentious matter altogether.

Hopkinson said, 'Well, of course, it should be short-crust pastry.'

Rick said, 'Well, I think it should be puff pastry.'

Bill Baker said, 'I think it should be a mixture of the two.'

And I said, 'Well, actually, I agree with Simon. It should be shortcrust, maybe with a hint of suet.'

And then something incredible happened. I saw Rick's face change. It went dark. Was he going to cry?

He suddenly stood up and said, 'Right the whole lot of you can fuck off out of my house. I never want to see any of you again. And as for making television programmes, David. It's finished!'

With that he stormed out of the kitchen and clunked up the stairs. I heard a slamming of the door, and that was that. We looked at each other in shock, and Bill, being Bill, opened another bottle of wine. To this day Rick and I never put the words pastry and Cornish pasty in the same sentence.

La dolce vita?

Chefs can be extremely temperamental. After I shot the first series with Rick, I must admit I did stray once. I made a series in Italy with Antonio Carluccio, during which I learnt a hell of a lot about Italian food, not least that nobody in Italy makes fresh spaghetti. It is always dried, and always al dente. We had never worked together before, and when I first met him, I thought this big bear of a man, with his roly-poly tummy, happy smiling face, and curly grey hair, talking passionately about olive oils of Liguria and the great dishes of Puglia and Sicily, encapsulated everything that was good about Italian food. How happy I was to be doing this series. And then we started working together.

These days (a far cry from those early, experimental days with Floyd) when you film a cooking sequence, you do it twice. The first time is the 'master shot', in which the viewer can see the whole scene: the kitchen, the person cooking, and the dish being made from beginning to end. Then you repeat it, this time filming only the food in beautiful back-lit close up: the garlic being chopped, the sausage frying, the wine being poured into the pot, because, after all, as Floyd used to say, the food should be the star of the show. Unfortunately, Antonio didn't understand this. Maybe I hadn't made myself clear at the beginning of the shoot.

We were in the kitchen of Milan's fashion school, where he was cooking lunch for some of the students, and with him was Gennaro Contaldo, his trusty second in command (since made famous in his own right by Jamie Oliver).

When I explained what I wanted to happen, Antonio said, 'No, no, no. I only do this once. You do your job. I do my job. I cook the thing. You film the thing. If you are not good enough to film it one time, I don't want to know.'

I listened to this tirade coming my way. I looked at the crew, who were melting into the walls of the kitchen, and thought, I can't have this. We were like rutting stags locking antlers. All this over a few spicy sausages cooked with wine and a bit of rosemary. It was so silly.

I wanted to say something entirely different, but what actually came out, in a very quiet voice, was something like this – and I still don't know where the words came from: 'I've got great respect for you Antonio, but when you are back in your restaurant walking around and being slapped on the back by customers who have paid lots and lots of money to eat your wild mushrooms, I will be stuck in some cutting room, trying to fit shots together that dignify you and your cooking. But *I won't have the shots*, Antonio. I won't have all the glorious detail that I so desperately need, and my editor will think, "You're not a very good director are you, David?" And I will be so woeful, so beside myself, that I may even give up television, because I won't want to do this any more. So I tell you what, Antonio, if you don't let me film this fucking sequence again, and I don't get my close-ups, I am going to tell my crew to pack up and go to Milan airport. We will fly off back home to England and leave you here, on your own.'

I looked at my crew and they knew I meant every word.

Antonio said, 'Gennaro, Gennaro, give me whisky now.' He drank the whisky and said, 'Pritchard, you are a bastard. But I will do what you say.'

I said, 'Thank you very much', and from that moment we got on fabulously well.

I am so pleased that we did because I learnt so much about Italian food from this man. He was a walking encyclopedia of gastronomy, although he did threaten to kill me with a roast duck in the town of Bussetto, the home of Giuseppe Verdi. To this day I am not quite sure how he intended to kill me with a roast duck, but the next couple of months working with him proved to be one of the most enriching filming experiences of my career.

The Emperor's clothes

Rick and I were in Tetsuya's restaurant in Sydney, which is famous for its experimental, fusion food. When you go in for a meal, you don't really get a meal, instead you get endless little plates and glasses of things, like tea and tomato soup, or a sliver of sea scallop with lemonade and yuzu, or cold spaghettini with sea urchin roe.

And they keep coming, one after another, looking ever so pretty, I grant you, but, 'What the hell is this?' I would say.

Then Tetsuya himself came out and Rick was telling him how fantastic and lovely everything was. And I was not saying anything, because in my book, the emperor wasn't wearing too many clothes here.

When Tetsuya had gone back to the kitchen, Rick admonished me. 'I think you were particularly ungracious,' he said. 'You didn't say anything about the food.'

'That's because I'm not impressed by it, Rick. I don't like things like this.'

'Well, I think you should open your mind to the efforts that so many chefs are making these days. This is very exciting.'

Rick and I have endless arguments like this, since he thinks my taste in food has barely moved on since the Seventies.

'Well, I'm hungry,' I said. 'I want lamb chops. I want gravy, and runner beans straight out of the garden, and new potatoes with mint sauce. And I want a cold glass of cider to go with it, too.'

I've been all over the world in the last twenty-five years and privileged enough to eat some amazing food. And I've learnt to make wonderful dishes, taught to me by experts: jambalaya at Joe Cahn's cookery school in New Orleans; a wonderful pasta dish with grilled red mullet, flaked into a sauce with fresh tomatoes, which Antonio Carluccio showed me; cassoulet, the definitive way, as explained to me by Keith Floyd. But I'm sorry, and I will argue this to the day I die, you cannot beat an English roast beef, Yorkshire pudding, spring greens, roast potatoes, and gravy.

When I go out to eat I don't want 'an experience', I want roast belly pork with apple sauce and mashed potatoes and local vegetables. I don't want tasting menus, or degustations. Degustations! Espresso-sized bowls of parsnip soup. What's that about? And foams! Have you ever tried foam? I have. I've tried prawn foam, actually. It tastes of frothy prawns. But what is wrong with a real prawn, I want to know. And it looks like the cuckoo spit you sometimes see on summer mornings on plants in the garden.

What is worse, these abominations have even found their way into pubs. I was sitting in the bar of my local pub not long ago, and the chef, who was all of eighteen, came out to have a Coca-Cola before he started his shift, so I thought I would make conversation.

I asked him, 'When you finish cheffing and you go home, what is the thing you most want to eat?'

He thought for a second and said, 'I think I would have a smoked salmon roulade. Yes, smoked salmon roulade with mascarpone; that would be really nice.'

I couldn't get it out of my head: a smoked salmon roulade? A swiss roll with smoked salmon and cream cheese. That's what you really want, is it? Not roast leg of lamb with mint sauce, or a good steak, even beans on toast, or sausages? A smoked salmon roulade. Well, there's no hope.

'Mind the …!'

Rick is the most accident-prone person I know. He's perpetually knocking his head or cutting his fingers and when it happens we will always be miles away on the estuary with no plasters handy. I can almost count him down to doing it.

Once, when we were filming him opening some blue clams in Southampton Water, using a huge knife, I said to the cameraman, 'We might as well start filming, but in fifteen seconds' time that knife is going to slip off the shell and he's going to stab himself and there will be blood everywhere.'

Sure enough, within moments of the camera turning over, Rick was shouting 'Ow! Ow!'

There will be a glass full of wine on the table; however, it won't be a glass full of wine for very much longer, because I can see that Rick is in expansive mode, and within minutes ... clunk, there it goes, smashing to the floor. What is so funny is that he always looks surprised.

'How did that happen?' he'll say.

By now the film crew will have that 'saw it coming a mile off' look on their faces, and he'll ask incredulously, 'How did you know I was going to do that?'

There are times when he is completely oblivious to what is going on around him.

I'll point something out to him, and he'll say, 'What? What? Where?'

'Too late, Rick.'

'What was it?'

'A dog with two heads, but never mind, Rick, it's gone now.'

Filming in Thailand, we were walking through some mushroom tunnels, dark, gloomy affairs with beams across the top and a plank in the middle to walk on in order to avoid the muddy floor. In Thailand the people are generally a bit shorter than we are, so, as the ceiling was so low, I was walking astride the plank, with my feet in the mud, to avoid hitting my head.

Rick came into the tunnel behind me, and I heard him say: 'Why aren't you walking on the pla—'

And then it went quiet. When I turned round, he was spark out on the floor. For four days we had to film him with a large scar on his head.

Another time in Thailand, we were filming on a beach, and I said to Rick, 'Just roll your trousers up and wander along looking nonchalant, a bit like Robinson Crusoe.'

The sea was coming in pretty strongly, but I said, 'Just walk along the edge.'

And then an almighty wave came from nowhere, right up to his waist, and nearly dragged him away. The hilarious thing is that in these situations, instead of reacting like a normal person would, he will try to act nonchalantly, a bit like a naughty child who thinks he can probably cover it up and no one will notice; even if he is waist-deep in water.

Filming out on a small trawler in the Solent, a fisherman was bringing up some rusted cannonballs in his net, covered in barnacles and bits of mud and clay. He had a good eye and he recognized that underneath they were actually Elizabethan cannonballs, so he started to bash them on the stern to get rid of the debris engulfing these heirlooms. And what did Rick do? He put his hand exactly where the fisherman was about to whack down the cannonball. Inevitably we heard an almighty shriek. Of course, he hadn't seen it coming.

But the most unnerving moment happened on a massive trawler off the north of Scotland. It was the size of a destroyer, and in truth, that was what it was: a huge fish-killer of a vessel, fitted up with computers and banks of screens which told the skipper where there was a shoal big enough to be scooped up in a net the size of a football pitch. The fish didn't stand a chance. In the old days, when we only had small boats, or drifters, thirty feet long, that allowed you to go out for a day, conservation was a natural thing; but now, to satisfy our greed, we have giant trawlers that can stay out for weeks and scoop up hundreds of tons of fish.

We shouldn't have been in the stern of the ship at all. I had been told by the skipper not to go down there because it was dangerous. There were ropes, cables, and chains, all constantly moving, and if you got caught up in one of those you'd find yourself in the sea, never to come up again. But having come this far, how was I going to get the shots I wanted if we had to film from the bridge? So I had taken my crew into this dangerous place. I shouldn't have done it. I know I shouldn't have done it, but you have got to get the pictures.

Rick, as usual, was oblivious to everything going on around him. He was leaning over the stern, looking at his Psion organizer – an ancient forerunner of the Blackberry – while he waited for us to start shooting. Suddenly, I heard an almighty grating noise, and with horror, I realized what was happening. The otter board was sliding on its chains towards Rick. Otter boards are flat pieces of metal weighing over a ton, which are designed to travel through the seabed, keeping the jaws of the net open. This one was speeding like a flying guillotine straight at Rick's head. I threw myself at him and pulled him over just as the otter board whistled past. How stupid, how utterly stupid I had been to allow Rick and my crew to be in this danger. I felt physically sick at the thought that in another second or so Rick could have been without a head. I crept away with my crew, like a timid little mouse, not wanting to film anything for the rest of the day.

'Bloody hell, Rick, you wouldn't be here if it wasn't for David,' said a white-faced Pete Underwood, the sound recordist, but Rick really hadn't a clue what a close shave he had had.

Cabin fever

I had bought a boat; actually my girfriend Jane bought it (did I mention that I was now separated from my wife Judith?). It was a brand new, gleaming twenty-six footer. It was a ridiculous thing to buy really, but, I thought, wouldn't it be lovely to meander along the canals in France, like a sort of big duck, stopping off at little bistros and bakeries and wineries, market towns and restaurants, passing villages by the back door. When you are in a car you always arrive via the industrial estates and the factories, and then you are in the centre of town, but from a boat you can see the pretty gardens of the houses and people fishing on the riverbank. What a great way to travel.

Rick and I were in a restaurant in Bristol called Le Quartier Vert, having had the most fabulous lunch of salt cod with roasted red peppers followed by a spicy Spanish stew made with chorizo, butter beans and rabbit. It was the sort of meal that goes really well with lots of inexpensive country wine. In fact, I would go as far as to say that the wine is as integral as the garlic, the rabbit and the chorizo sausage. We were in such good moods and when we're like this we naturally talk about what we want to do next. How about a boat trip through the canals of France? We could start at Bordeaux, potter down the Gironde to Toulouse, then on to the Canal du Midi, which would take us all the way to the Mediterranean where we would find fine oysters and, of course, the famous bouillabaisse of Marseilles.

The food would be our anchor, but what we would really be doing was exploring this wonderful region, discovering authentic dishes and meeting interesting people. I took out a pen, and on the paper tablecloth, around the splashes of wine, smears of butter and breadcrumbs, I drew a map of the south-west of France, and then a little boat on the canals, with Rick and Chalky in it. I drew in little matchstick farmers with artichokes or ducks, Chalky chasing free-range chickens, matchstick cheese-makers and fishermen. We wrote on the corner, 'This is what we want to do next, love from Ricky and David', folded it up, asked Barney Haughton, the owner of the restaurant, for a big envelope; and then, feeling enormously happy, went over to the BBC and handed it to the commissionaire, addressed to Tom Archer, my commissioning editor. If we hired my brand new gleaming boat, I thought, I could even have paid for maybe a third of it by the time we got back (shameful behaviour, I know).

It was possibly the first proposal the BBC agreed to that had no words, except for a few scribbles with arrows that said, 'nice ducks here', 'this cheese is worth tasting', or 'fancy some of those prawns', and it was certainly the first one ever presented on a tablecloth.

There was, however, a bit of a problem with my boat. In the sober light of day it was clearly too small. You could only put three people on it, four at a pinch, and apart from Rick and me we would have to house a film crew of at least five. It was my trusty old assistant, Frances, now a production manager at Denham's, who came up with the answer.

'Oh, David,' she said in her Scottish lilt. 'I read a holiday piece in the *Sunday Mail* about somebody who had gone through France on an old barge.'

I looked at the photo in the feature. The barge was 100 feet long, probably over a century old, black, red and white, and trustworthy. It was called *Anjodi* and I fell in love with it. There was a telephone number at the bottom of the article.

'How fast does it go?' I asked the owner.

'Well,' he said, 'you could walk quicker.' Perfect.

We had a little cabin, a little kitchen, loads of wine and we pootled along, watching the countryside slip past, through green tunnels of elms and spruces, through dappled sunlight and golden cornfields and villages where kids fished, past moorhens and blackberry bushes, on to the south, where the food was different, and there was a different smell in the air, of salt and sun, which grew hotter as the wine grew cooler, because people chill their red wines the further south you go.

Actually, it wasn't quite like that. At least, not at first. Normally when I am filming I have a rough jigsaw puzzle taking shape in my mind. At the end of each day I have a good idea of how things might come together in the cutting room; I might use this shot in a certain way, cut away to something else at this point. A particular poem Rick likes might fit in well with this scene, and then I'll phone Malcolm Ironton, the composer of the music for the series and a long-standing friend, describing the pace of the barge, the colour of the morning light, the mist over the passing vineyards. I will hear him scribbling it all down, so that later he can put these thoughts to music. But on this trip, every night I went to bed with doubts gnawing away at me, 'Have I been too rash here? Is this interesting enough?'

To make matters worse, I was sharing a cabin with my so-called best friend and fellow producer/director, Bernard Hall, who had come along to help with research. Also, we thought it would be good fun if he shot a little behind the scenes footage, which might end up as a separate programme. However, the camera had become a kind of symbol of moodiness. It began to annoy the hell out of Rick, because irritatingly Bernard never seemed to bring it out when everyone was happy and getting on; it always appeared when I was nervous and niggly or Rick was grumpy.

Bernard would crank things up for the purpose of his little documentary by saying to Rick, 'David is getting on your nerves, isn't he?'

And every night, without fail, he would repeat, like a relentless parrot on my shoulder, 'How can you sleep at night, David? Who is going to want to watch this rubbish; this old barge, looking exactly the same, day in, day out, with Rick looking around and cooking the odd sausage?'

So I would toss and turn, and then have nightmares in which the reviewers called me a profligate spender of the BBC's money, stretching out a programme which was barely interesting enough to make one half-hour's show let alone eight.

One night, sleepless and confused and needing air, I opened the porthole, using one of my precious Ecco walking shoes to keep it jammed open, and the shoe must have fallen out into the canal, because in the morning it wasn't there. My lovely comfy shoe belonged, not to me any more, but to the fishes. The great movie director, John Ford, was once asked by a student at film college, 'Mr Ford, what is the most precious thing a director can have?' And he said 'a comfortable pair of shoes'. And now, to add to my misery, one of mine had just slipped into the murky depths of the canal. This was a very low point indeed. I took the remaining shoe and cast it over the side.

'Join your friend,' I said with great sadness, as I watched it floating downstream.

And then I went back down to the cabin, and there, stuck down the side of Bernard's bed, was the other shoe. It hadn't fallen out of the porthole at all.

We were too cocooned together in a claustrophic space, that was the problem. We had breakfast, lunch, and dinner together, with our washing drying around us, and once the tide of unease set in, it rippled over everyone. There were times when Rick and I could barely speak to each other. Over breakfast the conversation would invariably go like this:

Rick/crew member: 'Is this going to be any good?'

Me: 'Yes, people are going to love it.'

Rick/crew member: 'But every day is the fucking same.'

After one of these conversations, when someone had said, 'What is there that is different or special about this programme, David?' suddenly everyone was looking at me.

It was quite a difficult question. I could have just said, 'I don't bloody know. Whose stupid idea was it anyway?' Mine? OK, another fine mess I'd got us into. But there are times when you have to be a bit of an actor in this game, you have to be able to turn on a performance when it really counts.

'What is special about it?' I boomed, puffing up like Orson Welles. 'What is special? Don't you *know* what's special about it? Don't you *realize* that we are living a dream, doing something that people at home with busy stressful lives would give their eye teeth to do, to travel slowly, to savour all the wonderful foods of France, to learn from the French how to make cheeses and wine and classic dishes.'

My soliloquy went on, along the lines of, 'You might *think* that every plant looks the same, but look again. Here are dog roses, there are wonderful purple irises sticking up out of the water. We'll go round a bend and there will be horses grazing and people tilling the soil. Soon we will come to Toulouse and we'll wake up and hear the traffic roaring past us and see the graffiti on factory walls. We'll be in this fine city full of markets and restaurants, which we'll go off and explore, and then we'll go through the fabulous Canal du Midi until we reach the Med.'

By now I was really enjoying my performance, and I thought I'd shift it up a notch. 'You could film all of this rich tapestry with no food, and it would still be interesting, but add on all the other layers: the farmers and the fishermen and the ingredients and the dishes, and mix the lyrical pictures with music, beautifully crafted by the composer, Malcolm, and a well-thought-out commentary, and we can take the viewers gently by the hand and lead them through France, and they will love it. Do you not see this as an opportunity to make a wonderful television series? Because *I* have no hesitation in saying this is going to be the best thing we have ever done. Mark my words.'

I wish I'd meant it.

'Wow,' said Rick and we went out to film with a spring in our steps.

And by the time I got into the cutting room, I did mean it. I thought, this is fantastic. Fortunately so did the viewers.

PART X

Reunited

Looking out of the window of the taxi taking me from Phuket airport to my hotel, I couldn't believe my eyes. I thought at first it was an advert for a stage version of *The Munsters*. There, caught in the car's headlights and at least twenty feet tall, was a slightly wizened and very hungover looking Keith Floyd dressed in chef's whites, proclaiming that food is lots of fun. I thought I must be caught up in a dream sequence and soon I'd wake up to find it was all the result of too much alcohol on the long, cramped flight. The taxi came to a stop at the traffic lights which gave me a moment to get the gist of this vast hoarding, an advertisement for Floyd's Brasserie in the Busari Hotel in the heart of Patong, a place that makes Benidorm look positively upmarket.

I'd seen pictures of Keith from time to time in the newspapers at home. Either he'd been banned from driving, or he'd been in the process of yet another divorce. Each time he'd looked somewhat more battered and frail than the last. Life, it seemed, was gradually catching up with the famous bon viveur.

It was sixteen years since we had last spoken, not counting the time we had met by chance in a pub, and he had accused me of implanting his character and sparkle into the television persona of Rick Stein. I told him I wasn't aware that I'd done any such thing, and even if it were possible, I don't think Rick would have been too happy about wearing someone else's personality when he has a perfectly good one of his own, one in which the ego is still fully intact and untroubled. Fortunately the bar was shutting by the time we had our pathetic little argument, but still the locals had to stand around finishing their beer, listening to a couple of idiots witter on about a stolen persona. And that was the last time I'd seen Keith.

Now I saw him staring down at me, proclaiming that food was fun.

'No, it's not, Keith,' I found myself saying out loud. 'Food stopped being fun for you years ago.'

'You know him. He your frien'?' the taxi driver asked.

'Yes,' I said. 'But that was a long time ago.'

Although our relationship had bordered on pathological hatred at times, the truth is I wouldn't be here, on a 'recce' mission to find locations to film in with Rick Stein, if it hadn't been for the mercurial Mr Floyd. He made me what I am today, as much as I made him, possibly more so because I knew very little about food when I started making these programmes. In short, I owed him.

I had vowed never to see Floyd again, but a friend had persuaded me that it was a preposterous situation to be writing about our relationship without actually meeting up with him again, and that it smacked of cowardice. The honourable thing to do would be to go to his brasserie

(French food with a Thai twist) to see if somehow we could put the past into context without killing each other in the process.

I thought I would surprise him by turning up unannounced, but when I arrived it turned out that the eagle had flown. Floyd had left Patong, and was back in rural France where he lived. Apparently, he only came over occasionally to make a guest appearance and he wouldn't be returning to Patong for several months. I thought of Provence, and our first day of filming there: the sunflowers, fields of lavender, the soft light, the food and cold red wine – a million miles from this place – and I felt quite wistful.

It would be several months before Keith and I were finally to meet up again.

Déjà vu

When I came back to Phuket several months later, after Rick and I had finished filming in Malaysia and Bali, the advertisement by the airport had gone. Where the picture of Floyd had been, there was now a vast expanse of rusty white steel plates waiting for a new customer. I knew Keith was here, because this time he had heard that I'd come looking for him and he had phoned me. Hearing that instantly recognizable sixty-a-day voice, made me feel at once nervous and elated. He had sounded extremely happy and proudly proclaimed he was drinking less. He said it as if the idea was a revelation, a breakthrough in medical science. I looked forward to meeting the new improved Floyd, but now the empty hoarding seemed like an omen.

The next morning, I walked the few hundred yards along the main road in front of Patong's busy beach front to the Busari Hotel. The pavements were packed, the air was putrid, and every two steps someone tried to sell me something. 'No thank you, I don't want a Rolex.' 'I already have a carved elephant.' 'I don't need a suit, or a set of duvet covers, or a hammock, or a fan', and 'No, I don't want a leaping tiger tattooed on my back.'

With relief, I reached the air-conditioned foyer of the hotel, and there, reclining on a leather sofa and surrounded by friends, was Keith.

'Pritchard,' he shouted. 'I don't know whether to punch you or give you a hug.'

He got up somewhat unsteadily. He looked tired and painfully thin and his custard cream-coloured trousers looked several sizes too big. But he seemed genuinely happy to see me and I thought then that coming here was the right thing to do.

The joy lasted for a few precious seconds, then: 'Don't think you're in for a smooth ride,' he warned, his eyes glinting like the hot coals of old. 'If it hadn't been for you, and people like you, I wouldn't be in this fucking mess in the first place.'

Sensing a shift in mood, his friends started to leave, one by one, until there were just three of us, the third being his new companion, an extremely jolly well-presented English lady in her early sixties who clearly doted on him.

Keith appeared to be drinking a large orange juice, so striving for a lighter tone I asked how his new alcohol-free regime was progressing.

He caught the eye of the waiter and signalled for another drink. 'In case you're wondering, these are large vodkas.'

'I am leaving this dump and I can't wait to get out,' he went on.

So that explained the empty advertising hoarding.

'Also, my wife and I are divorcing and after that I won't have a bean. My house in France, even my fishing rods, will be gone.'

There are times when Keith reminds me of a little boy standing at a crossroads with a hoop, while behind him is total carnage: piles of cars, smoking or in flames or ruins. And he's looking around bewildered, saying, 'Did I cause that?'

I felt sad, if not surprised. Twenty-five years ago this man had set the whole country talking. Like him or loathe him, he had revolutionized television cookery programmes, inspired people, men especially, to enjoy themselves cooking; he had even, ahead of his time, championed the cause of British food producers. But maybe, after all, he would have been a hell of a lot happier if he had stayed the flamboyant local hero in Bristol, cooking really good French food in his bistro, surrounded by friends and appreciative, if somewhat bemused, customers. Maybe he wouldn't have made much money, but he might have been a damn sight happier.

'They told me two days ago that my services would no longer be required,' he said, draining his glass. 'I was going to spend three months here. I was going to promote the restaurant, improve the menu, and hire some decent staff. Now, I've got no money, no job, and probably no home. It's just too much.'

Actually, I thought, the hotel owners might have done you an enormous favour. But I didn't say so. In times of trouble Keith always said that the best thing you can do is to drink yourself out of a crisis. And that is precisely what we did.

Some time later, after his new friend had tactfully popped out to do a spot of shopping, Floyd arranged for the hotel limo to drive the two of us back to his flat on the outskirts of Patong. The car stopped on a building site gouged out of the hillside skirting the city, next to a cement mixer churning away. The hot, humid air was thick with the noise of pneumatic hammers and angle grinders, overlaid with the incessant ping of reversing delivery trucks. A few buildings had been completed, and his turned out to be a relatively upmarket, low-rise apartment block.

'I hate this place,' he said walking up the steps. 'It's a living hell.'

From the balcony all you could see were high trees covered so thickly in bindweed it was impossible to make out the branches, but at least they screened the horrors of Patong.

As was his custom, Floyd announced he was taking a nap for an hour or so, and in the meantime I was to help myself to drinks. I sat and drank a couple more beers. It struck me that Floyd, when he was angry – which had been for most of the time since I arrived – would still make great television. I made a mental note to ask him what he thought about making one more programme together, a kind of TV version of Frank Sinatra's 'My Way'; or perhaps we should call it *Non, Je Ne Regrette Rien*. It would be a no-holds barred look at his life. And then I fell asleep.

An hour or so later, we made our way to a local hotel across a muddy building site. Curiously, everyone spoke French and it reminded me of a bar in Marseilles.

We had a few drinks, and in the unnerving way he always had of veering from mood to mood, he suddenly cheered up. He was like the old witty, charismatic Floyd that people adored. The Floyd who could walk into a room and everyone would stop and look, and he would hold them captivated with the *je ne sais quoi* of a Richard Burton, a Peter O'Toole, or Richard Harris. I remembered how he was so articulate, so debonair in his Aquascutum blazers and his bow ties. So funny at times, at others so fiery in his anger. He really did stand out. No one I knew could beat him at that game.

Even after sixteen years my emotions were all jangled up. I thought that there had been moments when I truly admired him, loved him to pieces, really; and equally there were moments when he would stir things up like the Joker in *Batman*, and though I'm not a violent man, I felt like I could have picked up a revolver, and this book, *Shooting the Cook*, might have been a completely different story: David Pritchard gets fifteen years for murder.

Keith had been right when he said, all those years ago, 'cooking is the new rock 'n' roll'.

'So what do you think of TV chefs today?' I asked him.

'I'd like to napalm the lot of them,' he said.

A bit extreme old boy, I thought, but actually I do agree. There are too many cooks on the telly and nearly every week I receive DVDs and letters from people whose sole aim in life is to be on TV and become a household name. Even when I go to pubs with restaurants I see young aspiring chefs in their flamboyant trousers that look like chequered flags – thank you to Gary Rhodes for that – and they all want to be Jamie Oliver or Gordon Ramsay.

'The other day,' said Keith, outraged, 'I saw this chap making a cassoulet on television – I don't know what his name was because once you've seen one you've seen them all – and it was a fucking travesty. And you know what, David, people like *you* are responsible. The trouble is, you people in charge haven't a clue about cooking, you know nothing about food, so you can't intervene and say "No, you don't do it that way", so these idiots get away with murder on TV.'

Here we go again, I thought, but he had a point because I know TV directors who wouldn't know a cassoulet from egg and chips. And the truth is, until I started working with Floyd I actually thought a cassoulet was a Pyrex dish.

He took a long drag from his cigarette, clearly enjoying the moment.

'Not only did this so-called TV chef use water instead of stock, but he used butter. A cassoulet is a work of simple genius. All the elements – the goose, the pork, the sausage, and the beans should be cooked in goose fat and

262

it is that, and the gelatinous pork rind, which gives it that unsurpassable velvety texture. To see these idiots using butter and water, it's like perpetuating a lie.'

Maybe, I suggested, we should get together one last time and show them how it should be done. I told him about the idea I'd had earlier in the day, about how we could call our swansong *Non, Je Ne Regrette Rien*, and to my surprise, he liked it. We shook hands, like we used to do in the old days when we had just hatched a new plan, and I was so overcome by the moment I gave him a kiss on the top of his head.

'David,' he said, and the old twinkle was back in his eyes. 'What *did* we unleash on the world? We should be thoroughly ashamed of ourselves.'

Acknowledgements

I felt like the pilot of a jumbo jet who had convinced himself he had run out of fuel, and then Sheila Keating came along, sat in the co-pilot's seat, pressed a switch and said, 'You've got loads of fuel left. Where do you want to go?' I can't thank her enough for helping me in my hour of need.

Thanks to Keith Floyd for being Keith Floyd; Rick Stein for being such a nice bloke and my best friend, and Bernard Hall for being my other best friend. To Antonio Carluccio, for opening the door to Italian food for me; to Lucy and Judith for bearing with me all these years; and, of course, Louise Haines, who had faith in me right from the very beginning, along with the whole team at Fourth Estate.

To Mark Thomas, the cover designer, who did the job I always wanted to do; everybody at Denham Productions who are like family to me; my poor, poor, long-suffering film editor Chris Waring, whom I have worked with for a quarter of a century; and the composer and my friend, the talented Malcolm Ironton.

Thanks to my film crews – you know who you are – my trusty assistants, Frances Wallis and Arezoo

Farahzad; and all the people in Filmingland, whose lives I have crash-landed into over the last twenty-five years, who have inspired me and helped make the programmes special. And Fiona.